BALTIMORE ORIOLES

60 YEARS OF ORIOLES MAGIC

BY
JIM HENNEMAN

INTRODUCTION BY
JIM PALMER

INSIGHT
EDITIONS

San Rafael, California

CONTENTS

INTRODUCTION
BY JIM PALMER

I t's been over fifty years since I started in the Orioles organization. I signed with the Orioles in the fall of 1963, but even in 1964 in my first year in Class A ball at Aberdeen, South Dakota, I still didn't really know the Orioles. They came to Aberdeen to play an exhibition game, and I didn't really know who Brooks Robinson was. I was born in New York and grew up a Yankees fan.

And then eleven years later, I got my first win against the Yankees. I came in to relieve Dave McNally. I even hit my first home run, off Jim Bouton. I went 30–16 lifetime against them, so I always liked beating them once I became an Oriole.

We moved to Los Angeles when I was young, and in 1963 the Dodgers beat the Yankees in the World Series. I was devastated, but I found out how good Sandy Koufax was. Who knew three years later I'd be facing him in the World Series? I beat Koufax, but that deserves an asterisk; he got the loss, but it really belongs to Willie Davis, who made three errors in center field that day for the Dodgers.

From California we moved to Scottsdale, Arizona, when I was a high school freshman. When I graduated in 1963, I had a lot of options to play baseball and basketball in college. I had played two years of American Legion ball, but Bobby Winkles, the baseball coach at Arizona State, suggested I play for Winner, a team that the Orioles sponsored in the Basin League, a college summer league in South Dakota. I was seventeen, the only high school player in the league, but I did well. Jim Russo would come up to scout the league for the Orioles, and I would drive him back to Pierre. I didn't know it, but he was getting to know me. Meanwhile, Jim Wilson, the Orioles scout in Arizona, was working on my parents. I ended up signing with the Orioles, and as it turns out, it was the best thing that ever happened.

PAGES 2–3: Brooks Robinson connects against the Reds in Game 3 of the 1970 World Series.
PAGE 4: As Alejandro De Aza steps in to face the Tigers' Max Scherzer, Adam Jones loosens up in the on deck circle at Camden Yards during Game 1 of the 2014 American League Division Series.
PAGES 6–7: Cal Ripken's 2,131st consecutive game, September 6, 1995.
OPPOSITE: The most heralded pitcher in Orioles history, Jim Palmer defined winning. In his 19-year career, all with the Orioles, Palmer won 268 games. He posted 20 or more wins eight times in a nine-year span from 1970 to 1978, won three Cy Young Awards, four Gold Gloves, and is the only pitcher to win a World Series game in three different decades. He went 8–3 with a 2.61 ERA in 17 postseason starts and earned first-ballot election to the Hall of Fame in 1990.

My first year in pro ball, we had a really great team at Aberdeen, high A ball at the time. I played for Cal Ripken Sr., and learned the Oriole Way, which really is: know everything you can about the game, have a great work ethic, go to the ballpark and get a little better every day, have fun, and have a passion for baseball. Cal Sr. was as instrumental as anyone in my development.

Robin Roberts, who went to the Hall of Fame, was my roommate when I made the big league roster in 1965. I was nineteen years old and sat in the bullpen. Sherm Lollar was our bullpen coach, and we had Dick Hall, Harvey Haddix, Stu Miller, Don Larsen. I got to see Milt Pappas and Steve Barber pitch. You had a lot of veteran guys you could glean information from. I used to keep Robin awake at night peppering him with questions. He'd say, "Kid, c'mon, you gotta let me go to sleep. I'm twice your age."

We were playing an intra-squad game at spring training in Miami in 1966, and Steve Cosgrove, who had an exploding fastball with a curve that fell off the table, threw Frank Robinson a curve. Frank kind of got out on his front foot but kept his hands back and hit a double right off the chalk down the left field line. I turned to Dick Hall and said, "I think we just won the pennant." And we did. Frank had that kind of impact.

As it turns out, a lot of guys got hurt in '66, so I had a chance to pitch and ended up winning 15 games. Dave McNally had a great second half; Eddie Watt, Davey Johnson, and Andy Etchebarren came up; and it was Paul Blair's second year—there were a lot of positive things. We still had a lot of pivotal players—Boog Powell had a great year, you've got Frank and Brooks Robinson, Luis Aparicio. We had a lot of guys who knew how to play the game.

> **" I played for Cal Ripken Sr., and learned the Oriole Way, which really is: know everything you can about the game, have a great work ethic, go to the ballpark and get a little better every day, have fun, and have a passion for baseball."**

Then Moe Drabowsky set the whole tone for the '66 World Series. McNally struggled in Game 1, but Drabo came in and strikes out 11 in six and two-thirds innings. He threw just fastballs, and the rest of us took our lead from that.

I tore my rotator cuff and missed most of '67 and '68. In 1968, Earl Weaver said in fall instructional league that he wouldn't give a nickel for my ever pitching in the big leagues again. In the instructional league, we had a hurricane come through the day of the expansion draft, so I didn't pitch. Teams could have taken me for next to nothing, but they didn't. I went to Caguas, Puerto Rico, and played winter ball. I went 6–0, pitched a no-hitter, and then went to spring training in 1969. That year I went 16–4 and led the league in ERA.

In the 1970s, we had McNally and Mike Cuellar, and we added Pat Dobson. Bobby Grich and Don Baylor came along, just a progression of really good players. We were in the mix the entire decade.

The one constant was the continuity of the organization. Sure, guys were coming and going—Harry Dalton, our general manager, left to go to the Angels, Frank Cashen took over and then left. We traded Frank. There was free agency—Reggie Jackson was here one year and left to go to New York. Nobody knew that free agency was going to be what it became. But we had good baseball people. Hank Peters came in as GM, and in 1976 we made the

great trade that changed our whole franchise, getting Rick Dempsey, Tippy Martinez, and Scott McGregor.

ABOVE: (From left to right) Jimmy Williams, Rick Dempsey, Tito Landrum, Jim Palmer, Ray Miller, and the Oriole Bird celebrated at city hall after winning the 1983 World Series.

Of course, Brooks Robinson was one of the constants. It's one thing if you're well known, beloved, on your way to being a Hall of Famer, which he was—I was just trying to figure out what I needed to do to stay in the big leagues. Guys like Brooks and Boog and others were good guys both on and off the field. These guys were talented, and they were civically minded. They got it.

Mike Flanagan used to say you don't want to get second-division players because most of the time they're always playing for the name on the back of their uniform, not the one on the front. That's their nature. We weren't a second-division team, so everybody was playing for the Orioles. You still had to have a good year individually to get your raise, but everybody was motivated to be on the same page, to play for the Orioles and not for Palmer or Robinson or Powell or whoever. It was a very special time because we had such great success and such great continuity. And we had Earl Weaver.

Earl was Earl. He didn't like to lose, and our players didn't like to lose. They had tremendous pride. My relationship with Earl was very simple: He gave me the opportunity to go out there and pitch and win all those games, and that's all you can ask of a manager. Now, did I want him to shake my hand, jump up, and give me a hug like Sparky Anderson did to Frank Tanana in the 1987 playoffs? Earl wasn't going to do that. First of all, he couldn't jump that high. And what was he going to do when you lost? But he was a very good baseball man.

One day, we came in from shagging, and Earl was going to give us a tutorial on pitching. A lot of people give me the credit, but it was Dave McNally who said, "Earl, the *only* thing you know about pitching is, it was tough to hit." And Mac got up, laughed, and we left.

Earl always had the same speech at spring training. "I'm going to take the best twenty-five guys, and if we play the way we're supposed to, we're going to win." It

didn't always work out, but we were always in it, always had a chance. One year, it's around the All-Star break, and we're like 42–48, and Earl says, "I made a mistake." And we're all like, geez, he's going to admit he made a mistake. And he says, "I picked the wrong twenty-five guys." Everybody started laughing. But that was Earl. He was another constant.

Earl fought for Eddie Murray to make the team in 1977 even though he was ticketed to go back to the minors. If you saw Eddie at spring training his first year, you could see he had talent. But watching batting practice, you'd say he had no chance whatsoever of playing in the big leagues. The worst batting practice hitter ever. Then the game would start. Eddie was a great athlete, and like others before him—it's really a common thread—he didn't like to lose. He wanted to do anything to make sure his team won. That was Eddie. That, and being one of four guys in history with 500 homers and 3,000 hits.

I met Cal Ripken Jr. in Aberdeen, South Dakota, when he was four and I was eighteen, and later he would come and work out at Memorial Stadium. In his first full season in 1982, Cal started out 7 for 60, but he figured it out. He took his natural ability and learned the baseball skills. By moving him to shortstop, Earl knew that Cal would figure it out because he's a really good athlete, and it would help our defense and our offense. Cal was another guy who did as much off the field as on it, who's had a tremendous impact on this community.

Today, Buck Showalter knows what he's doing, knows where he wants to go. He's utterly prepared, like Earl. He's very bright, a great organizer, a tremendous judge of talent, which is what Earl was. I still think one of the classiest things ever was Buck reaching out to Earl and understanding the Orioles tradition. The 2012 season was great in a lot of ways because the Orioles won 93 games, went to the playoffs, and we had the statue dedications. Earl went to all six of them. And so did Buck.

Are Buck and Dan Duquette, the vice president of baseball operations, going to agree on everything? No, and that's good. It's healthy. Earl didn't always agree with Harry Dalton, Frank Cashen, and Hank Peters. The point is for your vice president of baseball operations and your manager to have the same agenda, and that's to win.

I think winning is contagious, and Buck has created this environment of being prepared. I know it sounds trite, but the team under Buck "gets it." They want to walk off the field with a "W" and not a loss. Another similarity with Earl—although Buck may be more diplomatic, more tactful than Earl—is that he tells the players their job description, what he expects, and I think that's part of a winning environment. We signed guys all the time who came in and had to learn the Oriole Way. That has been revived by Buck Showalter. Call it Buck Ball or anything you want—it's playing the game the right way, having guys prepared, and putting them in position to win.

I get to do the Orioles on TV, in this park, with these great fans. On MASN, I work with Gary Thorne and Jim Hunter; Dawn D'Agostino, our producer, loves baseball, and the whole production crew really does a great job. The same thing applies to MASN as it does with baseball—we don't just show up and do these games. We have a game plan and storylines. It's like the Oriole Way: we're prepared.

So now, for me, it's been fifty years in the Orioles organization between pitching and broadcasting. I've never been anywhere else. Honestly, I can't imagine being anywhere else. I could have gone somewhere else to play and make more money. Instead, I did the underwear ads and stayed here. And now we've got one of the most beautiful ballparks, the prototype of all the modern-day stadiums. Baltimore is very comfortable, a great city. People really love the Orioles. They're interested in the team. People are wearing Orioles stuff, all the orange and black.

At Aberdeen in 1964, Cal Sr. said, "I usually have a one-dollar fine if you walk the opposing pitcher, but I think we have a good enough team so I'm rescinding that." And I thought great, because I could have walked anybody and I wasn't making that much money. Then Senior said, "Just remember"—and he looked up at the stands—"the reason we're here is because of the people that come out to see us play."

Has anything changed?

OPPOSITE: The Orioles signed thirty-five-year-old Robin Roberts on May 21, 1962, the same day he was released by the Yankees. In a little over three seasons with the Orioles, the one-time Phillies' Whiz Kid and future Hall of Famer went 42–36 and served as Jim Palmer's first roommate in 1965.

CHAPTER 1
BACK IN THE BIG LEAGUES

W hen the newly transplanted Orioles arrived home to play their first major league game in Baltimore in over half a century, the pregame routine was hardly routine.

"We came in on an overnight train from Detroit, where we had opened the season," said Bill Hunter, the shortstop on the 1954 Orioles, "and we were herded like cattle into a waiting caravan of cars."

It became clear very quickly that this wasn't going to be like any other opening day for Hunter, one of the three young stars (along with pitchers Bob Turley and Don Larsen) branded as building blocks for a franchise that relocated from St. Louis following the 1953 season. Long before infield practice, there would be a full dress parade on a six-mile route through downtown Baltimore to Memorial Stadium on 33rd Street.

"It's kind of ironic looking back," said Hunter, "that our train came into Camden Station, just a few hundred feet from where the team now plays. We had gotten dressed into our game uniforms on the train, and I'm not even sure how our street clothes got to the ballpark."

After spring training in Yuma, Arizona, and two games to open the season in Detroit, the Orioles were finally home, and the city was eager to embrace them. A light rain fell throughout the morning, but more than 350,000 people lined the streets anyway, as schools and businesses closed to welcome Major League Baseball back to Baltimore for the first time since 1901.

From Camden Station, a parade of floats and twenty-two marching bands joined a cavalcade of cars carrying players, staff, owners, city and state dignitaries, and Vice President Richard M. Nixon, who would later throw out the ceremonial first pitch. North on Howard Street, east on Baltimore Street, north again on Charles Street, and up to Memorial Stadium they went. It took a full hour and a half for the final float to get started in the parade.

"I just remember being ushered into a car and seeing heads sticking out of office windows and people lined up along the streets all the way to the stadium," Hunter said. "It was quite a scene, really. I said to Vinicio Garcia, who was riding in the car with me, 'I wonder what they would do if we won.'"

OPPOSITE: Crowds line the streets as the Orioles parade from Camden Station to Memorial Stadium for their first home game, April 15, 1954.

The Orioles did win that afternoon, beating the Chicago White Sox, 3–1, before a packed stadium that was still being worked on, with scaffolding and paint crews and carpenters working to bring the facility up to major league caliber.

But victories would be few and far between for the Orioles that first season and for several years thereafter. Like Memorial Stadium itself, it would take some time for the home team to complete its makeover and leave the remains of the hapless St. Louis Browns behind. For the team's fans, as well as for Bill Hunter, who was traded after the '54 season and later returned as an Orioles coach, it would be a dozen years before they found out "what it would be like if we won."

Today, sixty years later, Memorial Stadium is long gone. The Orioles play in a retro-style ballpark that has influenced every other baseball facility built for more than two decades, one that sits next door to the very train station that launched not only that first parade but also World Series championships, Hall of Fame careers, and so many moments that would come to be described as "Orioles Magic."

In 1954, however, the wins and losses didn't matter as much as the simple fact that Baltimore was back in the big leagues.

If it can be said that "the Great Fire of 1904" forever changed the city's landscape, then it can certainly be documented that an early July 4 ballpark fireworks display forty years later fanned the flames of hope for the return of Major League Baseball to Baltimore.

Without the massive 1904 fire that ravished 1,500 buildings, spanned seventy city blocks, devoured what is now the downtown waterfront, caused a staggering $150 million of damage, and took 1,231 firefighters from as far away as New York more than two days to control, Baltimore would have survived as a city—but perhaps not as progressively as it did in the aftermath of the devastation.

There's little doubt, however, that when errant fireworks set aflame "old Oriole Park" during the morning hours of July 4, 1944, it set in motion a dramatic chain of events that would put Baltimore into the American League in less than ten years—though few could have envisioned it at the time.

After the 1904 tragedy had paralyzed his city, Mayor Robert McLane was quoted in the *Baltimore News* as saying, "We shall make the fire of 1904 a landmark not of decline but of progress." Less than three years later, on September 10, 1906, the *Baltimore Sun* reported that the city "had risen from the ashes and one of the great disasters of modern times had been converted into a blessing."

OPPOSITE TOP: Manager Jimmie Dykes on the train ride from Detroit to Baltimore for the Orioles' first home opener on April 15, 1954.

ABOVE: General manager Art Ehlers (left) and manager Jimmie Dykes (right) lead the parade from city hall to Memorial Stadium before the first home opener, April 15, 1954.

ABOVE: (From left to right) General manager Art Ehlers, manager Jimmie Dykes, and club president Clarence Miles at the Orioles' first spring training in Yuma, Arizona, in 1954.

> *Disaster would be converted into a blessing yet again when the burning of the antiquated minor league stadium in 1944 put Baltimore on a return path to the big leagues."*

Disaster would be converted into a blessing yet again when the burning of the antiquated minor league stadium in 1944 put Baltimore on a return path to the big leagues. Just as the fire that leveled a city had a national impact in 1904, so too did the burning of the minor league ballpark forty years later.

The national implications weren't immediately obvious when the minor league baseball team was left without a home, but by the time World War II ended, Baltimore had exploded onto the scene as a major league candidate after the minor league Orioles found the unlikeliest of homes.

When their park was reduced to a pile of ashes, the Orioles lost every piece of team equipment. All that remained were road uniforms, which had been sent to the cleaners—and would be worn exclusively for the next couple of weeks while officials scrambled to find a suitable place to play. "Old Oriole Park," officially dubbed Oriole Park V because it was the fifth one to carry that name, was bounded by Greenmount Avenue, 29th, 30th, and Barclay Streets in a northeastern part of town that was equal parts business and residential.

Not much more than a mile away as a bird flies was Municipal Stadium. Horseshoe-shaped and with a capacity in excess of 60,000, it was better suited for football and only months away from hosting the Army-Navy game for the second time. It too was an all-wooden structure, with bench seating and a configuration not suited for baseball. But it was available, and as city and team officials would soon learn, it was the best thing that could've happened for the future of baseball in Baltimore.

What were initially meant to be temporary arrangements were hastily made with city officials. Owner Jack Dunn III was on duty with the army, so it was left for the team business manager Herb Armstrong and groundskeeper Mike Schofield to quickly install a diamond and turn Municipal Stadium into a makeshift baseball facility. The result was a ballpark conducive for three things: short home runs to left field, where the distance was generously listed at 260 feet; long fly ball outs to mammoth right and center fields, where distances initially ranged beyond 500 feet; and huge crowds. When the minor league Orioles returned to settle into their new home, they would see an abundance of all three.

Setting the stage for an improbable season, the minor league Orioles christened their new home by playing four consecutive doubleheaders against the Montreal Royals, the top farm team of the Brooklyn Dodgers, winning eight straight games in the process. With the area heavily populated with defense workers and military personnel from nearby bases, Municipal Stadium was suddenly transformed into a popular gathering place, and crowds in the 20,000 to 30,000 range became routine—highly unusual for minor league baseball.

Instead of a disaster that seemed to doom their season, the ballpark fire launched the Orioles on a magical ride. The old park was quickly relegated to its place in history, and the team's fortunes would be dramatically altered over the next five and a half years.

Outfielder "Howitzer Howie" Moss would benefit the most from the "short porch" in left field, finishing that initial season with 27 home runs. After missing a year to service, he hit a total of 124 homers from 1946 to 1948. Moss would finish his career with 279 minor league home runs.

Riding the wave of an unprecedented attendance surge, the Orioles clinched the 1944 International League pennant on the last day of the season and went on to defeat Louisville in the Junior World Series. It was Game 4 of that series, ironically a 5–4 loss, which changed the face of baseball in Baltimore forever.

A crowd of 52,833 showed up for that game, over 20,000 more than for any of the sold-out games of the 1944 all-St. Louis World Series between the major league Browns and Cardinals. After that, a return to the big leagues became more than just a dream. Rodger H. Pippen, sports editor of the *Baltimore News-Post*, had championed the cause of a new stadium ever since the fire.

"What appears to be a baseball tragedy may turn out to be a blessing in disguise," Pippen wrote. "Baltimore rose from the ashes of its great fire in 1904 to be a bigger and better city. Our Orioles will come through just as soon as war conditions permit, with a bigger and better place for their games. The new park will be built so in case the opportunity should arise, this city will return to the big leagues. The park which is today in ruins was not suitable for big-league competition."

After the war, in 1946, the Orioles' season attendance soared to nearly 700,000. Future big-league stars like Sherman Lollar and Eddie Robinson were making their mark, and Baltimore was drawing national attention. Pippen and Mayor Tommy D'Alesandro Jr. stepped up the crusade, and by 1949, with the Orioles playing games in the horseshoe end of Municipal Stadium at 36th Street, construction began at 33rd Street on what would become Memorial Stadium.

When the minor league Orioles moved for the 1950 season, Memorial Stadium was still a single deck with seats from foul pole to foul pole, and it would remain under construction until its double-deck completion four years later. At the time, the minor league Orioles were in the last year of a two-year working agreement with the Browns—and, as it would develop, four years away from inheriting the parent team as its own.

BELOW: The National League Orioles of the 1890s won three straight pennants and produced a number of future Hall of Famers, including manager Wilbert Robinson.
OPPOSITE: Orioles stars of the 1890s included (clockwise from top left) future Hall of Famers Willie Keeler, John McGraw, Hughie Jennings, and Joe Kelley.

O's EARLY ORIOLES

Even before its return to the American League, Baltimore had a rich heritage in professional baseball with teams that were both colorful and successful. The long and storied history is virtually unbroken dating back to the years shortly after the Civil War. Along the way a couple of dynasties were formed— in addition to the one started inadvertently by the transfer of the original American League franchise to New York.

It all started in 1872 when a team named the Canaries joined the National Association of Professional Base Ball Players. The team was often called the Yellow Stockings for the obvious reason and usually referred to in box scores as the Lord Baltimores. That team lasted only two years, replaced in 1874 by the Maryland Base Ball Club. By the following year, the league itself had folded.

In 1882 a team formally named the Lord Baltimores became a charter member of the American Association, a newly formed major league to rival the established National League. A year later the team adopted the name "Orioles," which began the association between Maryland's state bird and Baltimore's professional baseball team that remains intact to this day.

While the Orioles and the American Association struggled for acceptance, two other professional teams formed in Baltimore in 1884, but neither would survive the year. One team, in the Union Association, was also named the "Orioles" and transferred in midseason to Lancaster, Pennsylvania. The other, called the "Monumentals," became a charter member of the Eastern Association, which would ultimately become the International League, but it disbanded after only 13 games.

In this era, teams and leagues were in a constant battle for survival, and there was often joint ownership. The Orioles and the American Association were in similar dire circumstances. The team dropped out in 1889, only to return a year later to replace the Brooklyn Gladiators, the first but not the last time the cities would be linked.

What happened next could be described as the final indignity for what very well might have been the most storied team of the nineteenth century. Denied the chance to retire the Temple Cup when the series was discontinued, the 1898 Orioles team found itself dismantled when most of the team's stars, with the exception of John McGraw and Wilbert Robinson, were transferred to the Brooklyn Dodgers by the joint ownership of the two clubs.

Despite a fourth-place finish in 1899, the Orioles were one of four teams eliminated by the National League, leaving Baltimore without a team until McGraw followed through on his threat to abandon the National League. He formed a franchise for Baltimore in the newly formed American League in 1901 (initially named the Orioles), but the team would last only two years before moving to New York, where the team changed its name from the Highlanders to the Yankees and became the most dominant team in history.

During this era, franchises and players often moved about with abandon, not burdened by lengthy contracts or leases. Following the Orioles' move to New York, Ned Hanlon, one of those who had been dispatched to Brooklyn, tried to convince his partner, Charles Ebbetts, to move to the vacated Baltimore territory. When Ebbetts refused, Hanlon bought Montreal's Eastern League franchise and moved it to Baltimore, starting a minor league Orioles team that would last half a century.

The league would eventually become the International League, and the Orioles would become its most dominant team.

After the 1950 season, the Browns attempted to move to Milwaukee but were rebuffed by the Boston Braves, whose farm team was located there and who, in 1953, would move there themselves. Bill Veeck had bought the Browns, and he next tried, unsuccessfully, to move them to Houston and later to Los Angeles.

Baltimore attorney Clarence W. Miles became Mayor D'Alesandro's point man for Baltimore's bid to acquire the Browns, whose lagging attendance was forcing Veeck's hand. After the 1953 season, the flamboyant owner proposed selling a half-interest in the team that would have left him in control, but the American League rejected that offer. New York Yankees owner Del Webb was the principal objector, arguing that the Washington-Philadelphia corridor already was saturated with Major League Baseball.

However, after two more votes on a proposed move failed, Veeck closed on a deal with Miles and the family of Jerold C. Hoffberger, owner of the National Brewing Co.: Veeck would sell the team in whole to Baltimore interests, and to appease Washington Senators owner Clark Griffith, the brewery would become a major sponsor of the Senators. The American League owners hastily approved the sale and transfer, and on September 30, 1953, D'Alesandro and Miles emerged from the meetings in New York to celebrate Baltimore's return to the majors.

The fire that burned "old Oriole Park" to the ground a little more than nine years earlier had indeed proved to be the spark that ignited the city's big league dreams.

CHAPTER 2
THE FIRST YEAR

Bob Turley

The euphoria of gaining a major league franchise was quickly replaced by the reality of putting together an organization. Only a handful of the team's nonplaying personnel, the most prominent being the minor league director Jim McLaughlin, made the move from St. Louis, so team president Clarence Miles was charged with quickly assembling a front office staff and field manager.

Arthur Ehlers became the team's first general manager, and he named Jimmie Dykes as manager. The two had a previous working relationship with the Philadelphia Athletics, so it made for a comfortable pairing for the initial season—but one that ultimately would not survive beyond the first year.

Little, however, could dull the excitement as Baltimore prepared for its first major league game in fifty-two years. Even with the team training far away in Yuma, Arizona, the air back home filled with anticipation as Ehlers and Dykes held out hope that the Orioles would be competitive, despite the Browns' 54–100 record the previous year.

Hope for improvement centered on young prospects like shortstop Bill Hunter and pitchers Bob Turley and Don Larsen, along with veteran pitchers Joe Coleman and Duane Pillette, outfielder Vic Wertz, third baseman Vern Stephens, colorful catcher Clint Courtney, and second baseman Bobby Young, a Baltimorean who had been purchased from the minor league Orioles after the 1950 season.

The team headed to Detroit for a two-game series to open the season. Then they returned to Baltimore for an elaborate home-opening reception, and everyone wondered what impact, good or bad, the expansive outfield dimensions of Memorial Stadium would have on the team. It wouldn't take long to find out.

OPPOSITE: Bob Turley, who threw the first big-league pitch ever at Memorial Stadium, went 14–15 and led the AL in both strikeouts and walks in 1954.
FOLLOWING PAGES: Clint Courtney is all smiles after the Orioles' first-ever home run in their home opener, April 15, 1954.

BOB CHAKALES

GIL COAN

JOE COLEMAN

CLINT "SCRAP IRON" COURTNEY

VERN STEPHENS

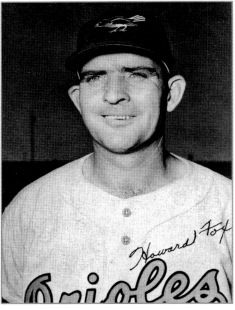

HOWIE FOX

JIM FRIDLEY

LOU KRETLOW

DICK KRYHOSKI

Don Larsen

The home opener against the Chicago White Sox could hardly have gone better. Turley showed why he was considered the ace of the staff, pitching a complete game seven-hitter and striking out nine in a 3–1 win."

The home opener against the Chicago White Sox could hardly have gone better. Turley showed why he was considered the ace of the staff, pitching a complete game seven-hitter and striking out nine in a 3–1 win. Fitting the occasion, Baltimorean Ed Rommel was the home-plate umpire, and Young, the local product who had also been the Orioles' first modern-day big-league hitter in the season opener in Detroit, was the home team's leadoff hitter.

Then, in what would turn out to be a misleading scenario, Clint Courtney homered in his first at-bat in the third inning, and the very next inning Stephens also connected, both blasts coming off losing pitcher Virgil Trucks. It was not a scene that Memorial Stadium would see replayed often.

The Orioles would hit only 52 home runs for the season, with Stephens the top contributor with eight. Even though the Orioles outhit the opposition by a scant .251 to .250 margin, they would struggle to score runs throughout the year, eventually being outscored 668–483. While Cal Abrams (.293), Stephens (.285), and Courtney (.270) posted respectable batting averages among the regulars, the Orioles were almost devoid of power.

The dimensions at Memorial Stadium were a deceiving 309 feet down the foul lines, and a staggering 447 to the gaps in left and right, and 450 to straight

OPPOSITE: Of the nine players pictured, only Coan, Fox, and Kretlow lasted beyond the '54 season, and all were gone by 1956. Coan got the Orioles' first-ever base hit, a single on April 13, 1954, in the opener at Detroit, and Courtney hit the first homer in the home opener two days later. Stephens, a veteran whose best days were behind him, led the club with eight homers and 46 RBIs in their first season. Coleman went 13–17 in his lone season with the team. Fridley and Kryhoski were part of a seventeen-player trade with the Yankees following the '54 season.

ABOVE: Don Larsen, the first starting pitcher in club history, lost the season opener in Detroit and went on to lead the AL in losses, going 3–21. Traded to the Yankees following the season as part of a seventeen-player deal, he went on to pitch the only perfect game in World Series history with New York in 1956. Larsen rejoined the Orioles in 1967 as a reliever.

THE DUNN DYNASTY

In 1907, four years after future Hall of Fame manager Ned Hanlon bought the Montreal team of the International League and moved it to Baltimore, he lured the manager of the Providence team, Jack Dunn, to take over the minor league Orioles. Hanlon couldn't have known it at the time, but in hiring Dunn he put in motion a series of events that would result in one of the biggest dynasties in minor league baseball history.

Dunn, who would continue as a player-manager through 1911, bought the team from Hanlon after the 1909 season. The owners of the Philadelphia Athletics—Connie Mack, and John and Tom Shibe—were minority investors, and so a steady stream of players flowed between the two teams until 1914, when the ill-fated Federal League, which stole players from the existing American and National leagues but lasted only the 1914–1915 seasons, made an appearance in Baltimore.

That was the same year Dunn signed Babe Ruth, who made his professional debut on April 22, pitching a six-hit shutout before only 200 fans. In dire need of cash, the owner/manager offered Ruth to Mack, who deferred, saying he couldn't afford what he knew the Babe was worth. Mack directed Dunn to Joe Lanin, who owned the Boston and Providence teams, setting the course for baseball history when Ruth's contract was sold to the Red Sox.

While the Federal League played out its existence, Dunn moved the team to Richmond before returning to Baltimore in 1916 and proceeded to put together a mostly home-grown team that would win seven straight International League pennants from 1919–1925. Only the San Francisco Seals of that era were said to have as many local performers as Dunn was able to assemble for the Orioles.

Third baseman Fritz Maisel and shortstop Joe Boley played on all seven pennant winners—with six of the those teams later acclaimed to be among the 35 best minor league teams of all time (the 1921 team was the highest ranked at number two). The 1926 team would finish in second place, but the Orioles won 100 games for an unprecedented eighth straight year, capping an era that would never again be repeated.

For Dunn personally, however, triumph was mixed with tragedy. His son, Jack Jr., who was being groomed to take over operation of the team, died suddenly of pneumonia in 1923 at the age of twenty-seven. Five years later, at the age of fifty-six, Jack Sr. died of a heart attack. Jack Sr.'s wife then controlled the team until, fifteen years later, grandson Jack III inherited it and, after finishing a tour of duty in the army, took over as president and general manager. Later, Jack III even served as interim manager after he fired Tommy Thomas midway through the 1949 season.

When the American League's St. Louis Browns came to Baltimore in 1954, Jack Dunn III sold the International League franchise to a Richmond group, retaining the Orioles' name for the major league team. He was a member of the new big league team's front office for twenty-four years, serving in capacities of traveling secretary, public relations director, radio commentator, and vice president for business affairs until his death in 1987. His son, Jack IV, the great-grandson of the patriarch of the Dunn Empire, is an investor in the Orioles' ownership group, giving the organization four generations of Dunn family baseball tradition.

away center. These dimensions were particularly devastating to Wertz, who saw most of his best-hit drives caught on the warning track. After hitting 19 home runs for the Browns in 1953, and having a string of 20 or more home runs for four straight years before that, Wertz became the symbol of the power hitters' frustrations at Memorial Stadium.

On June 1, after only 29 games, 94 at-bats, one home run, and compiling a .202 average, Wertz was traded to the Cleveland Indians in exchange for right-handed pitcher Bob Chakales. Ehlers traded Wertz probably as much out of sympathy as an effort to help the club.

With offense not a factor in that first year, pitching accounted for whatever success the team found, though Larsen had a tough time believing that. Larsen started 28 games and lost all but seven of them, finishing with a 3–21 record. His 4.37 earned run average was the only one among the four top starters to exceed 3.50.

The other starting pitchers helped make up for Larsen's tough first year. Turley wound up leading the league in both strikeouts (185) and walks (181), while posting a more-than-respectable 14–15 record and 3.46 ERA. Coleman finished 13–17 (3.50 ERA), and Pillette was 10–14 (3.12 ERA).

Five pitchers on the inaugural team started at least 20 games, with sixteen pitchers in all being utilized. This included left-hander Jehosie Heard, who pitched in two games and became the first African American to play for the Orioles on April 24, 1954. Almost five months later, on September 10, Joe Durham made

OPPOSITE TOP: Vice President Richard Nixon throws out the first pitch at Memorial Stadium on April 15, 1954, signaling Baltimore's return to the major leagues after fifty-three years.
OPPOSITE BOTTOM: Memorial Stadium, as it looked on opening day 1954. The box seats would not be extended until the 1961 season.

his debut as the club's first African American position player, and he would become a lifelong Baltimore resident.

The Orioles' record that year ended up the same as the one the Browns had in their last year in St. Louis, 54–100, but it was enough to advance one spot in the standings and end the season in seventh place. In their first year the Orioles' attendance reached 1,060,910, which was the fifth highest in the American League.

Cal Abrams ended up the leader in the club's meager offensive totals, leading the team with a .293 average, 124 hits, and 67 runs scored. In addition to his eight home runs, Vern Stephens led the team with a modest total of 46 runs batted in, while Chuck Diering's defensive work in center field, in addition to a workmanlike .258 batting average and 108 hits, earned him the distinction of being named the first Most Valuable Oriole.

The biggest news of the year came in the season's last month when it was revealed that a deal had been negotiated for Paul Richards, who had an interesting track record with the minor league Orioles, to take over as the club's manager-general manager—a surprising move that would signify a new era just one year after Baltimore had returned to the major leagues.

After the news that he was being relieved of his duties broke, Jimmie Dykes was given a day in his honor on September 15, perhaps the only manager ever to be honored after he'd been fired. It capped a "Welcome Back to the Big Leagues" season for the Orioles.

THE NEGRO LEAGUES IN BALTIMORE

During three decades from the 1920s through the 1940s, Baltimore was represented by two teams in the Negro baseball leagues—the Elite Giants and the Black Sox. Most of the great Negro league players who are now recognized in baseball's Hall of Fame played with or against one or both of these teams. For instance, two future stalwarts of the Dodgers, James "Junior" Gilliam and Roy Campanella, whose Hall of Fame career would end tragically due to injuries following a 1958 car accident, both played two different stints with the Elite Giants.

" Almost five months later, on September 10, Joe Durham made his debut as the club's first African American position player, and he would become a lifelong Baltimore resident."

RIGHT: Signed out of the Negro leagues in 1953, Joe Durham came over with the Browns and was called up in September 1954. On September 12, he became the first African American to homer for the Orioles. After two years in the army, he spent part of the 1957 season with the Orioles, and later served more than thirty years with the club as a minor league coach, batting practice pitcher, and community ambassador.

MEMORABLE GAMES
1954

April 13, 1954

Following their transfer from St. Louis after the 1953 season, the Orioles play their first game, losing 3–0 at Detroit. Gil Coan singles for the first of seven Orioles hits, and Don Larsen takes the first of his 21 losses during the season, still a club record.

April 15, 1954

After a fifty-one-year absence, Major League Baseball returns to Baltimore as a crowd of 46,354 watches the Orioles beat the White Sox, 3–1, in the first game played at Memorial Stadium. Bob Turley is the winning pitcher, and Clint Courtney and Vern Stephens hit home runs.

April 14, 1954

The Orioles win their first game ever, 3–2 at Detroit, as pitcher Duane Pillette goes the distance. The O's score three runs in the first inning. Maryland native Bobby Young doubles and scores the club's first run on Gil Coan's single.

July 30, 1954

Bob Kennedy's bases-loaded home run off New York's Allie Reynolds—the first grand slam in Orioles history— keys a 10-0 win over the Yankees at Memorial Stadium. In their 39th home date, the Orioles top the best season attendance ever by their predecessors, the St. Louis Browns, whose high mark was 712,918 fans in 1922. The Orioles have drawn over 720,000 at this point.

CHAPTER 3
THE RICHARDS ERA

T he parade that welcomed the Orioles to Baltimore in 1954 was a celebration that ran through the heart of town. A year later, a less-happy parade occurred, as players marched in and out of the clubhouse at a furious pace.

Paul Richards, baseball's first manager-general manager since John McGraw, was the grand marshal as the Orioles set a tone for change months before spring training. Richards left no doubt that a complete roster makeover was his first order of business. His "revolving-door policy" resulted in an 80 percent turnover in personnel in the first year.

The "Richards Era" might best be noted for its steady procession of high-profile and often low-performance "Bonus Babies"—amateurs signed to big-dollar contracts who were required to stay on the big league roster instead of getting seasoning in the minors—who put a serious dent in the club's bank account but added few wins to the scorebook. There were some notable exceptions, particularly Brooks Robinson and Milt Pappas, but the theory of quantity begets quality paid minimal dividends, especially in the early years of the Paul Richards regime.

While the abundance of Bonus Babies was his early trademark, Richards's signature move came barely three months into his Baltimore career. With one trade, Richards emptied the Orioles' roster of its three most prominent names—pitchers Bob Turley and Don Larsen and shortstop Bill Hunter. Consternation over this among fans was compounded by the fact that Richards sent the trio to the perpetually hated Yankees.

The trade was so elaborate and complex that it took two weeks to complete as the teams moved players on and off major and minor league rosters. Confusion lingers today, as the trade is still sometimes referred to as an eighteen-player deal, but only seventeen names are listed.

The original announcement was for a three-for-six player deal: the Orioles sent their three premier players to the Yankees for pitchers Harry Byrd and Jim McDonald, outfielder Gene Woodling, shortstop Willy Miranda, and minor league

OPPOSITE: New manager Paul Richards (left) and pitching coach Harry Brecheen (right) go over the pitching rotation in 1955.

prospects Gus Triandos (first baseman/catcher) and catcher Hal Smith. The second part of the trade saw the Orioles send pitcher Mike Blyzka, catcher Darrell Johnson, first baseman Dick Kryhoski, and outfielder Jim Fridley to New York in exchange for pitcher Bill Miller, second baseman Don Leppert, third baseman Kal Segrist, and minor league outfielder Ted del Guercio.

The mammoth trade pleased Richards a lot more than it did the fans—so much so that he boldly predicted the Orioles would make a dramatic improvement in the standings. "I think we can now be absolutely considered as first division challengers," he said. "It's tough to trade someone like Turley, who can be a great pitcher, but you can't win with one pitcher who goes out once every four days."

The merits of the deal would be heatedly debated over the next few years, but eventually it became clear that the Yankees benefited most. Triandos emerged as the Orioles' only star performer, while Turley won a Cy Young Award in 1958, and Larsen pitched a perfect game in the 1956 World Series and then was used in the 1959 trade that brought Roger Maris to New York. However, not all of Richards's trades were in vain.

In retrospect, the big trade was easily overshadowed by a move Richards made shortly after the 1954 season. In that deal, little-used infielder Vinicio "Chico" Garcia went to the Dodgers in exchange for Ray Moore, a hard-throwing right-handed pitcher. Richards also bought veteran pitcher Jim Wilson from the Braves, who went 12–18 and made the All-Star team for the Orioles in 1955.

OPPOSITE TOP: Willy Miranda was a light-hitting shortstop but a marvel with the glove. Acquired from the Yankees as part of a seventeen-player trade after the 1954 season, he spent five seasons with the Orioles.
OPPOSITE BOTTOM: The first incarnation of the Oriole Bird—known as "Mr. Oriole"—made its debut in 1955 but did not last. A mascot would not return until 1979.
ABOVE: Players gather around new manager Paul Richards (No. 12) during spring training 1955 in Daytona Beach, Florida.
FOLLOWING PAGES: Whether talking to his players or a group of youngsters, manager Paul Richards didn't smile a lot.

Gene Woodling, whom Richards would label his "bitterest disappointment" from the Yankees trade, was gone before midseason (though he would return three years later and be a contributor). The Orioles were so offensively challenged in 1955 that Dave Philley, who hit .299, was the team's "Most Valuable Oriole" despite playing in only 83 games.

The most significant development during Richards's first year was the signing of a teenage infielder (originally a second baseman) from Little Rock, Arkansas. After breaking in with two strong months with the York White Roses, Brooks Robinson made his major league debut with the Orioles, collecting two hits in his first game and then going hitless in 18 additional at-bats the rest of the way—though he would be heard from again.

The '55 season set the stage for the rest of Richards's seven-year tenure in Baltimore. That year, the Orioles used a total of fifty-four players, including nineteen starting pitchers, club records that still stand even after six decades of play.

Undeterred by that season's modest three-game improvement (increasing from 54 to 57 wins), which didn't meet the team's lofty preseason expectations, Richards embarked on an instructional program that included minor league managers, coaches, and scouts and introduced film sessions along the way. He was a strong believer in teaching—especially his young Bonus Babies, of which there were many. It was not uncommon for the younger players to be summoned for morning workouts after night games as Richards tried to hasten the learning process.

Among the higher profile youngsters signed during his era, there were more misses than hits. The 1955 team featured four of the Bonus Babies—Jim Pyburn, Tom Gastall, Bob Nelson, and Wayne Causey—along with Bruce Swango, Dave Nicholson, and Brooks Robinson, who was the only impact position player developed in that stretch. However, pitching was Richards's strong suit and signees Milt Pappas, Billy O'Dell, Chuck Estrada, Jack Fisher, Steve Barber, and Jerry Walker provided the pitching depth that would ultimately blossom into the "Kiddie Korps" that led the O's surge in the 1960s.

In 1956, while he continued to support a strong youth movement, Richards also took advantage of the waiver wire and trade market. On May 21, 1956, one year after picking up Jim Wilson and Dave Philley with bargain buys, he traded them to the White Sox for third baseman George Kell, outfielder Bob Nieman, and pitchers Connie Johnson and Mike Fornieles. It would prove to be one Richards's shrewdest moves.

Kell became the perfect mentor for Brooks Robinson, and he also provided help at both third and first base; Nieman was the Orioles' best hitter; and Johnson was a solid three-year starter. The trade gave the Orioles—the worst-hitting team in baseball at the time—decent offensive potential. Triandos emerged as a legitimate power threat, with 21 home runs, Bobby Boyd (a preseason purchase) hit .311, and Nieman finished with a .322 average as the Orioles approached respectability with a 69–85 record.

One year later, in 1957, with Connie Johnson leading the pitching staff with a 14–11 record, the Orioles' record reached .500 for the first time. They wouldn't be able to maintain this over the next two years, but it was an inkling of promise for the future. In 1957, Richards also determined that Robinson would "work in gradually," as Kell moved between third and first.

During those early years, the Orioles were the highest spending team in baseball when it came to amateur free agents (this was before the amateur draft, which started in 1965). With only paltry immediate results, ownership made an effort to restrain Richards, bringing in Bill Walsingham Jr. as an executive vice-president. But the former head of the St. Louis Cardinals' front office was no match for Richards, who started on his second three-year contract in 1958 when Walsingham's less-than-two-year tenure ended.

In 1958, the All-Star Game was held in Baltimore for the first time. The American League's 4–3 win was notable primarily for the absence of extra-base hits by either team. Billy "Digger" O'Dell made it a big day for O's fans when he pitched three scoreless innings, retiring all nine batters and winning the game's MVP Award.

OPPOSITE: Eddie Robinson, here instructing Dave Nicholson, joined the Orioles as a coach in July 1957 and was activated and played in four games. He coached again in 1958 before moving into the club's minor league department.
ABOVE: Not yet established as "No. 5," Brooks Robinson flashes some of the form that made him a Hall of Fame third baseman during spring training in Scottsdale, Arizona, in 1957.

Perhaps Richards's most brilliant personnel move was his last as the team's manager-general manager. On August 23, 1958, the Orioles claimed Hoyt Wilhelm on waivers from Cleveland. Already thirty-six years old, the knuckleballer had logged only six starts in his previous 391 games, and it's hard to imagine that even Richards could've known what would follow.

In 1958, Wilhelm made four more starts for the Orioles, three of them complete games. The second was a 1–0 no-hitter against the Yankees on September 20, with the Orioles' lone run coming on Gus Triandos's 30th homer of the year, at the time an American League record for catchers. Instead of his career entering its twilight stage, Wilhelm pitched for another twelve years and a total of 679 more games. It is not an exaggeration to suggest that Richards salvaged what became a Hall of Fame career.

OPPOSITE TOP: Outfield candidates pose during spring training in 1956: (first row from left to right) Joe Cristello, Joe Duffy, Jim Pisoni, Angelo Dagres, Bill Lajoie, Bob "Tex" Nelson; (back row from left to right) Tito Francona, Chuck Oertel, Dave Pope.
OPPOSITE BOTTOM: Chuck Diering and Tom Gastall horse around in spring training in Scottsdale, Arizona, in 1956.
ABOVE: First baseman Bobby Boyd, nicknamed "Rope" for the line drives he hit, batted over .300 in four of his five seasons with the Orioles, 1956–1960.
TOP RIGHT: Long before he became a Hall of Fame manager, Dick Williams played five seasons with the Orioles from 1956 to 1962. He is one of three men to be acquired by the club on three different occasions, along with Elrod Hendricks and Harold Baines. As manager of the Oakland A's, he lost to the Orioles in the 1971 ALCS before winning the World Series the next two seasons.
ABOVE RIGHT: Connnie Johnson joined the Orioles in May 1956 in a six-player trade with the White Sox and went 29–30 over two and a half seasons. He went 14–11 with a 3.20 ERA in 1957.

Prior to the 1959 season, the organization was feeling the effects of friction between Richards and the minor league director Jim McLaughlin, and Lee MacPhail was brought in to be general manager. In making the announcement, team president Jim Keelty said, "Paul Richards is the best manager in baseball." True or not, this was an obvious attempt to divert attention from the fact that Richards was being relieved of his general manager duties. There was little doubt that the Orioles felt the organization was best served with Richards in the dugout rather than in the front office.

After reaching .500 in 1957, the Orioles slumped to 74 wins in 1958, and by the end of the 1959 season, MacPhail's first as general manager, the results were identical, 74–80. The Orioles got off to a quick start in 1959, and on June 9, they were tied for first place. But the next night Rocky Colavito of the Cleveland Indians set a Memorial Stadium record with four successive home runs, leading the Indians to an 11–8 win, and this started the O's on a downspin that ended with them in sixth place.

Hoyt Wilhelm was easily the highlight of the '59 season. He made 27 of his 52 career starts that year, finishing with a 15–11 record and a 2.19 earned run average that led the American League. The Orioles generally fared well against the better teams, especially the pennant-winning White Sox. Their 11–11 record versus the

White Sox included five extra-inning games, two of which went 17 innings and one bizarre contest that ended after 16 innings.

That game was the second game of a doubleheader at Memorial Stadium on September 11, and it produced probably the most remarkable pitching performance in team history. In the first game, Jack Fisher won a 3–0 duel over Chicago's Billy Pierce, and then Jerry Walker pitched the entire 16 innings of the second game, allowing only six hits, as the O's completed the shutout doubleheader sweep with a 1–0 win.

The 16-inning game was played in three hours and forty-seven minutes, less than an hour longer than an average game lasts today, and Walker threw a staggering 188 pitches. "One of the best efforts I can remember, and I qualify it only because I saw the great Carl Hubbell beat the Cardinals, 1–0, in 18 innings [in 1933]," said Richards, who wasn't concerned about the number of pitches Walker had thrown. "It wasn't that many for 16 innings," he said. "It was cool, his shirt wasn't even wet, and he didn't seem tired."

In 1959, at the age of twenty, Walker became the youngest pitcher to start an All-Star Game. His final record that year was 11–10, but in 1960 Walker went only 3–4 in 18 starts. Then, before the next season, he was traded to Kansas City, and Walker pitched his last major league game September 25, 1964.

OPPOSITE: (Clockwise from top) Acquired in late May 1956 from the White Sox, outfielder Bob Nieman went on to win Most Valuable Oriole honors, hitting .322 with 12 homers and 64 RBIs. His .303 batting average in three-and-a-half seasons (1956–1959) is third in club history; one of the few veterans among the Orioles "Kiddie Korps" of pitchers in the late fifties and early sixties, Hal "Skinny" Brown spent eight of his 14 big league seasons in Baltimore, winning 62 games from 1956–1962; Al Pilarcik spent four up-and-down years as an Orioles outfielder after being acquired from the A's after the 1956 season; acquired early in 1956, George Kell spent the last two seasons of his fifteen-year career with the Orioles, ostensibly brought in to help tutor a young fellow Arkansan, Brooks Robinson, at third base. Kell nonetheless represented the Orioles in the All-Star Game both seasons, batting .261 and .297. In 1983, he was elected to the Hall of Fame—along with Robinson.

ABOVE: Billy "Digger" O'Dell gets congratulations from Yankees shortstop Tony Kubek after earning the save in the 1958 All-Star Game at Memorial Stadium. O'Dell retired the last nine National Leaguers in order to preserve a 4–3 victory.

One reason why Walker made only 18 starts is 1960 was the emergence of starting pitchers Jack Fisher; Chuck Estrada, who led the league with 18 wins; and Steve Barber, who made the jump from Class D minor league ball to join Milt Pappas and Hal "Skinny" Brown in the regular rotation, with Hoyt Wilhelm moving to the bullpen. Jim McLaughlin, the minor league director, had coined the phrase "home grown by '60," and he would see it come to fruition, as ten products of the minor league system made the team by that year. However, General Manager Lee MacPhail decided McLaughlin and Richards could no longer coexist, and in the middle of the 1960 season, MacPhail let McLaughlin go and promoted Harry Dalton to the position of farm director.

In every sense, 1960 was a breakthrough year for Richards and the Orioles. Ron Hansen, who had been stymied twice by injuries, took over at shortstop; Robinson became entrenched at third base after making his last minor league stop the year before; Jim Gentile, obtained from the Dodgers over the winter, became a force while being platooned at first base; and Marv Breeding hit .267 as a steady second baseman. Outfielder Gene Woodling's career had been rejuvenated since he returned to the Orioles for the 1958 season, and in 1960 he hit a solid .283 and gave the young lineup a veteran presence.

The remarkable turnaround kept the Orioles in the pennant race until the middle of September. Going into New York for a four-game series, the Orioles

OPPOSITE TOP: Lee MacPhail (left) was brought in as general manager in 1958, leaving Paul Richards (right) as the field manager only.

OPPOSITE BOTTOM: Jerry Walker was one of the "Kiddie Korps" of young pitchers signed out of high school in the late 1950s by the GM/manager Paul Richards. He pitched four seasons for the Orioles (1957–1960) began the '59 season 7–3, and was the AL's starting pitcher in the All-Star Game at age twenty.

BELOW: Jerry Walker, part of the Orioles' "Kiddie Korps."

RIGHT: Gus Triandos (left) congratulates Hoyt Wilhelm (right) after the knuckleballer no-hit the Yankees, 1–0, on September 20, 1958. Triandos's 30th homer of the season was the difference in the first no-hitter in Orioles history.

BOTTOM: Paul Richards brings his lineup card to home plate before his first home game as Orioles manager, April 12, 1955.

OPPOSITE TOP FAR LEFT: Willie Tasby, the Orioles centerfielder in 1959, once played in stocking feet on a rainy afternoon rather than risk his metal cleats getting struck by lightning.

OPPOSITE TOP MIDDLE: Marv Breeding started at second base as a rookie in 1960, but after two seasons of part-time play he was dealt to the Senators and was out of the majors after 1963.

OPPOSITE TOP RIGHT: Chuck Estrada, part of the "Kiddie Korps" of pitchers in the early 1960s, tied for the league lead with 18 wins as a rookie in 1960.

OPPOSITE BOTTOM: Jack Fisher pitching in relief during his major league debut, April 14, 1959. Part of the "Kiddie Korps" of pitchers, he went 30–39 in four seasons with the Orioles and gave up Ted Williams's final home run in 1960 and Roger Maris's 60th homer in 1961.

ABOVE: Swing and a miss! Gus Triandos in action at Memorial Stadium in 1959.

LEFT: Gene Woodling was practically run out of town in his first go-round with the Orioles in 1955, hitting .221 in 47 games before being traded to Cleveland. Reacquired in a trade three years later, he went on to have three productive years for the club and was Most Valuable Oriole in 1959, when he batted .300 with 14 homers and 77 RBIs. He coached first base from 1963 to 1967.

O's PROFILE GUS TRIANDOS: THE FIRST SLUGGER

Without question Gus Triandos was the most polarizing player of the Paul Richards era. Big and burly, he hit home runs, struck out and grounded into double-plays with a degree of regularity that kept him front and center when it came to fans' not-always-constructive criticism.

An affable guy who was widely liked and respected in the clubhouse, he hit 142 home runs during his eight years with the Orioles, the all-time leader at the time of his departure following the 1961 season, when he and Whitey Herzog were traded to the Tigers for Dick Brown. Although he originally broke in as a first baseman his first season, Triandos would eventually become an All-Star catcher and set an early American League record for home runs by a catcher, with 30 in 1958.

While it was offense that generated most conversations about Triandos, it was his defense that was most overlooked, especially after Hoyt Wilhelm joined the Orioles in '58. Wilhelm's dancing knuckleball was responsible for Triandos twice leading the league in passed balls. Unfortunately it would become his signature defensive statistic—overshadowing one that should have established his defensive excellence.

Possessor of a strong and accurate arm and a fast release, Triandos set an early standard for defending against the stolen base. In 1957, ironically, the year before Wilhelm arrived to torment him, Triandos threw out forty-two of sixty-three runners who attempted to steal—an unheard of 67 percent. For his career, Triandos caught 189 of the 390 runners who tried the stolen base route—a remarkable .484 percentage that would command attention years later, but go relatively unnoticed during his career.

He got notoriety for all the wrong reasons, but Triandos was one of the best defensive catchers of his time.

were tied for first place with the Yankees, who then swept the O's in a well-played but unrewarding series. Despite the fact that the Orioles rebounded strongly to win six of their last nine games, including five of the final six, they finished eight games behind the Yankees. Still good enough for a second-place finish, their 89–65 record stamped them as contenders for the foreseeable future and marked a 15-game improvement over the previous two years.

Robinson established himself as a rising star and finished third in the Most Valuable Player voting, two spots ahead of Ron Hansen, who won Rookie of the Year honors in a season when at least two other Orioles teammates warranted serious consideration. As it was, five Orioles—Hansen, Gentile, Breeding, Estrada, and Barber—were named to the All-Rookie team.

The revolving-door policy was no longer in effect. The job was not finished, but the Richards Era was getting close to the goal. The only question, as the 1961 season approached, was whether or not the architect would be around to see the final product.

OPPOSITE: Billy Gardner (No. 9) handled second base for the Orioles from 1956 to 1959, leading the league with 36 doubles in 1957.

TOP: The Orioles' first legitimate home run hitter and early folk hero, Gus Triandos had a street named in his honor in Timonium, Maryland. He tied an AL record with 30 home runs by a catcher in 1958 on the same night he caught Hoyt Wilhelm's first Oriole no-hitter, winning 1–0.

RIGHT AND FOLLOWING PAGES: After brief call-ups in '58 and '59, shortstop Ron Hansen broke into the starting lineup in 1960 and won AL Rookie of the Year honors, hitting 22 homers with 86 RBIs. He started two more seasons for the Orioles before being traded to Chicago in a deal that netted Luis Aparicio.

MEMORABLE GAMES
1955–1960

September 17, 1955

Eighteen-year-old Brooks Robinson, in his first pro season, is recalled from Class B York of the Piedmont League and goes 2-for-4 with an RBI in his big-league debut, a 3–1 win over Washington before an attendance of 5,486 at Memorial Stadium. In five more games that season, the future Hall of Famer goes 0-for-18 with 10 strikeouts. Twenty-two years and one day later, nearly ten times as many fans will pack Memorial Stadium for "Thanks, Brooks Day."

September 20, 1958

Knuckleballer Hoyt Wilhelm pitches the first no-hitter in Orioles history, beating the New York Yankees, 1–0, at Memorial Stadium. Gus Triandos's 30th home run—at the time an American League record for catchers—accounts for the game's only run.

May 18, 1957

With seconds remaining before a prearranged 10:20 p.m. curfew to allow the White Sox to catch a train to Boston, Chicago's Paul LaPalme only has to hold the ball or throw it wide to leave with a win. Instead, Orioles first baseman Dick Williams hits the first pitch of the ninth inning for a home run to tie the game at 4–4 and force the game to be replayed in its entirety at a later date.

June 9, 1959

The Orioles beat Cleveland, 7–3, before 46,601 fans at Memorial Stadium to tie the Chicago White Sox for first place. It is the first time in the Orioles' six seasons that they have been in first place after the second day of the season.

July 8, 1958

Memorial Stadium hosts its first and only All-Star Game. The Orioles have two players on the American Leaguae squad—starting catcher Gus Triandos goes 1-for-2, and reliever Billy "Digger" O'Dell is the hero, retiring the last nine National League batters on 27 pitches for a save and earning the unofficial MVP Award. Baltimore native Eddie Rommel, a thirteen-year pitcher and twenty-one-year umpire in the majors, calls balls and strikes.

September 11, 1959

In the second game of a doubleheader at Memorial Stadium, Jerry Walker pitches a club record 16 innings to beat the White Sox, 1–0. Walker allows six hits and three walks, and Brooks Robinson's two-out single scores Al Pilarcik to give the O's a doubleheader sweep. Jack Fisher's complete-game three-hitter wins the first game, 3–0. Exactly fifteen years later, Ross Grimsley gets a no-decision while pitching 14 innings against New York; no Orioles pitcher has gone longer since.

August 28, 1960

The Orioles lead the White Sox, 3–1, behind Milt Pappas before Chicago's Ted Kluszewski hits a three-run homer in the eighth inning to put the Sox ahead. But third-base umpire Ed Hurley calls time just before the pitch because two Chicago players (Earl Torgeson and Floyd Robinson), who are preparing to enter the game defensively, are warming up outside the bullpen area in Memorial Stadium's foul territory. With the homer negated, Kluszewski flies out to end the inning, and the Orioles go on to win, 3–1.

July 9, 1959

A pair of twenty-year-olds, Milt Pappas and Jerry Walker, toss complete game shutouts as the Orioles sweep the Senators, 8–0 and 5–0, in a doubleheader at Washington's Griffith Stadium. Before the doubleheader, twenty-two-year-old Brooks Robinson rejoins the club from AAA Vancouver and never returns to the minors.

July 15, 1960

Brooks Robinson becomes the first of four Orioles to hit for the cycle, going 5-for-5 with 3 RBIs in a 5–2 win at Chicago's Comiskey Park. Robinson singles in the first and fifth innings, homers in the third, and doubles in the seventh before completing the cycle with a ninth-inning triple.

May 27, 1960

Clint Courtney uses an oversized catcher's mitt designed by Manager Paul Richards to help handle Hoyt Wilhelm's knuckleball. Wilhelm goes the distance and Courtney does not commit a passed ball in the Orioles' 3–2 win over the Yankees. Courtney's glove—one-and-a-half times the size of a standard catcher's mitt and about 40 ounces heavier—is later outlawed by baseball's rules committee.

CHAPTER 4

EXPANSION AND A CHANGING OF THE GUARD

The euphoria of the Orioles' out-of-nowhere charge into the 1960 pennant race carried over to the following season, when banners and bumper stickers proclaimed "It Can Be Done In '61." However, that year Major League Baseball also entered into an expansion era for the first time, and the American League added two teams: the Washington Senators (replacing the team that moved to Minnesota and became the Twins) and the Los Angeles Angels. Thus, before a ball was put in play, there were signs that improvement in 1961 would be hard to define.

Before they reported for spring training, the Orioles lost nine players from the organization. Outfielders Chuck Hinton and Gene Woodling, pitchers Dean Chance and Ron Moeller, infielders Billy Klaus and Don Ross, and catcher Gene Green were taken in the expansion draft by the Senators and Angels, while outfielders Leo Burke and Albie Pearson went to the same teams via the minor league draft.

If the system that spurred the "Home Grown by '60" slogan proved to be fertile ground for the American League's expansion teams, that didn't dull the Orioles' expectations for the coming season—and there was early evidence that

OPPOSITE: Fans line both sides of Howard Street as the Orioles make their way to Memorial Stadium during the 1961 opening day parade.

the team was ready to roll. Coming off his breakthrough year, Brooks Robinson had his salary doubled—to $20,000—an indication that great things were expected. Jim Gentile was poised for a big year, which he set in motion by being the first player ever to hit grand-slam home runs in consecutive at bats in a 13–5 win at Minnesota on May 9. Plus, the "Kiddie Korps" rotation of Milt Pappas, Steve Barber, Chuck Estrada, and Jack Fisher was intact for the second straight year. But success in 1961, as it turned out, would have to be defined by individual progress rather than team advancement, as expansion appeared to have tilted the balance of power in favor of the more established and powerful teams.

The first ominous note was sounded on opening day, when Pappas lost a 7–2 decision to Eli Grba and the expansion Angels. Through the first half of the season, that seemed only a blip on the screen: the Orioles made a remarkable run up to the All-Star break, and it appeared the Orioles were on the verge of something special.

They went 16–4 during a 20-game streak, which included a stretch of 72 innings when the pitching staff allowed only five earned runs for an ERA of 0.61. Sitting with a 48–37 record at the All-Star break, the Orioles were in good position for a second-half run, but the tables quickly turned. They suffered eight losses in the first 11 games coming out of the break, which set the tone for the rest of the season.

Even though the Orioles would finish with their best record ever at 95–67, they would slip a spot in the standings to third place, 14 games behind the Yankees, who cruised to a 109–53 record, and six games behind the Detroit Tigers, who finished 101–61. The drop in the standings overshadowed the team's general improvement—and some strong individual accomplishments.

Freed by Richards from his former role as a platoon player, Jim Gentile exploded to win the team's batting triple crown with a .302 average, 46 home runs, and a league-leading 141 runs batted in. He also led the team in runs (96), walks (96), on-base percentage (.423), and slugging percentage (.646), completing a remarkable year that was easily the best of his career. Despite the general rise in offensive numbers, the pitching staff finished with a team record low 3.22 ERA. In his second year, Barber finished with an 18–12 record and a league-high eight shutouts.

Despite these individual accomplishments and the team's overall improvement, which produced the most wins in club history, much of the second half of the season centered on Richards and whether he would return to manage for an eighth season. MacPhail pushed for a decision in early September, when it was announced that Richards would step down immediately and take over as general manager for the newly formed Houston Colt 45s (a National League expansion team whose first season would be 1962). Paul Richards's tenure in Baltimore ended with a 517–539 record (.490), but the 100-loss team he inherited his first year would finish his last year with 95 wins, an accomplishment that would earn him induction into the Orioles' Hall of Fame in 1984.

The 1961 season still had 27 games to go, however, and third-base coach Luman Harris jumped in as interim manager (compiling a 17–10 record). Lee MacPhail wanted to move quickly away from the "Richards Era," and less than two weeks after the conclusion of the 1961 season, Billy Hitchcock was named as the Orioles' new manager. Yet Hitchcock's first season did not go as planned.

In 1961, the escalation of the Berlin Crisis resulted in several Orioles players being called into military service, limiting their availability for the 1962 season. Most notably, shortstop Ron Hansen, a steady contributor in 1961, was limited to part-time duty, and pitcher Steve Barber, an 18-game winner in 1961, was relegated to the role of "weekend warrior" for much of the season.

OPPOSITE TOP: Despite his pitching background, Luman Harris spent four years as the White Sox third base coach under Paul Richards, then joined him in the same position in Baltimore from 1955 to 1961. In September 1961, when Richards re-signed as Orioles manager to become GM of the new Houston franchise, Harris was named interim manager and guided the club to a 17–10 mark—his .630 percentage is the best in club history.

OPPOSITE BOTTOM: Robin Roberts delivers to the Tigers' Norm Cash on July 1, 1962, at Memorial Stadium.

TOP: Pitchers gather around pitching coach Harry Brecheen at Memorial Stadium in 1962: (from left) Hoyt Wilhelm, Wes Stock, Dick Hall, Hal Brown, Billy Hoeft, Steve Barber, Milt Pappas, Chuck Estrada, and Jack Fisher.

LEFT: Dick Williams is tagged out by Yankees' first baseman Moose Skowron in a game on August 26, 1962. Williams batted .255 in five seasons with the Orioles.

FOLLOWING PAGES: Future Hall of Fame manager Whitey Herzog, here scoring against the Tigers on July 1, 1962, batted .280 in two seasons with the Orioles.

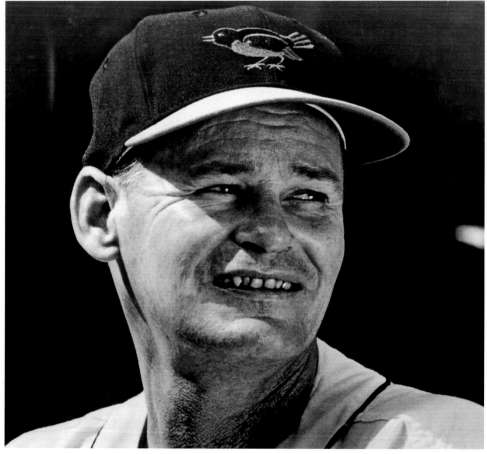

Before he ever got acclimated, the season seemed to get away from both Hitchcock and his team. With Barber in the service and Milt Pappas and Jack Fisher both nursing sore arms, Chuck Estrada was the only dependable starter and everything quickly went downhill. The tone was set early, on May 5, when Barber lost a 2–0 game to the Angels, as ex-Oriole farmhand Bob Belinsky pitched a no-hitter.

Other than winning 11 of 18 games in their season series against the Yankees, the Orioles accomplished little as they plunged to a 77–85 record and a dismal seventh-place finish in 1962. Estrada, who two years before had topped the league with 18 wins, now led with 17 losses.

The following off-season might have been the most tumultuous in team history, as MacPhail was intent on remaking the team's image. In a sign of what was to come, the GM influenced a makeover of Hitchcock's coaching staff and then made two trades that would drastically affect the roster. Coaches Cal Ermer, George Staller, and Darrell Johnson (one of the players involved in the famous trade with the Yankees) were dismissed. Pitching coach Harry Brecheen was the only holdover, as Luke Appling and Hank Bauer were added to the staff.

The makeover of the coaching staff proved to be minor in comparison to what happened to the roster. On November 26, Gus Triandos got a belated

OPPOSITE TOP: Coach Luke Appling talks to a group of pitchers at spring training in Miami in 1963: (front row from left) Pete Burnside, Mike McCormick, Steve Barber, and Dean Stone; (back row from left) Dave McNally, Frank Bertaina, Bill Short, and Steve Dalkowski.

OPPOSITE BOTTOM LEFT: In 1962 the Orioles turned to longtime Tigers coach and minor league manager Billy Hitchcock to manage the club. Hitchcock compiled a 161–161 record in two seasons before being reassigned as minor league field coordinator in 1964.

OPPOSITE BOTTOM RIGHT: Before he became a symbol of the hapless expansion New York Mets, Marv Throneberry began the 1962 season with the Orioles. "Marvelous Marv" batted just .190 in 65 games over parts of two seasons with the Birds before being traded to the Mets on May 9, 1962.

ABOVE: During the 1964–65 seasons, Jerry Adair set the major league record for second baseman for fielding percentage (.994) and fewest errors (5), both of which would be surpassed by future Oriole Bobby Grich.

Thanksgiving present when MacPhail traded him along with outfielder Whitey Herzog to the Detroit Tigers in exchange for catcher Dick Brown. Less than a month later, on December 15, MacPhail further rearranged the catching staff when he sent pitchers Billy Hoeft and Jack Fisher along with newly acquired catcher Jimmie Coker (from the Phillies a month earlier) to the San Francisco Giants for catcher John Orsino, left-handed pitcher Mike McCormick, and relief ace Stu Miller.

Those trades set the stage for the bombshell announcement on January 14, 1963, when shortstop Ron Hansen, infielder Pete Ward, outfielder Dave Nicholson, and pitcher Hoyt Wilhelm were dealt to the Chicago White Sox in exchange for shortstop Luis Aparicio and outfielder Al Smith. This bold move eventually worked for both teams, but the Orioles gave up a lot of talent to add, by acquiring Aparicio, the missing element of speed to the lineup. Over

OPPOSITE: Acquired from the Giants with pitchers Stu Miller and Mike McCormick in December 1962, John Orsino shared the catching duties in the first half of the '63 season with Dick Brown and Charlie Lau before catching fire in mid-season, batting .295 with 15 homers from July 3 to the end of the season.
ABOVE: Luis Aparicio was acquired from the White Sox and spent five seasons as the Orioles shortstop from 1963 to 1967. He twice led the league in stolen bases and had 166 in his Orioles career.

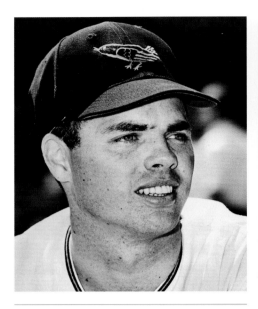

ABOVE: Bob "Rocky" Johnson played all four infield positions as well as left field in four seasons with the Orioles from 1963 to '66, averaging 83 games a year and batting .254, before being sold to the Mets early in the '67 season.

RIGHT: One of the last players to come out of the Negro leagues, Sam Bowens hit 22 homers and drove in 71 runs as a rookie in 1964. He was never the same hitter after being hit by a pitch in spring training in 1965.

the next two seasons, Aparicio would lead the league in stolen bases, including a still club record of 57 in 1964.

Although that trade would not return the immediate dividend hoped for, MacPhail felt it gave the Orioles a dimension that was unmatched. In *My 9 Innings: An Autobiography of 50 Years in Baseball,* MacPhail observed: "With Aparicio at shortstop and Brooks Robinson at third base, I honestly think that's the best left side of the infield that's ever existed in baseball." That no doubt was a contributing factor to what became pitcher Steve Barber's best year: he finished the 1963 season as the first 20-game winner in team history, compiling a 20–13 record and 2.75 ERA.

The "new look" on offense didn't pay off, however, as the Orioles' team batting average increased only one point to .249, and run production dropped from 652 to 644. The 86–76 record in 1963 was a nine-game improvement over 1962, but it was not nearly enough to salvage Billy Hitchcock's job, as he was replaced as manager by Hank Bauer at the end of the year. And that wasn't the only significant change. With his numbers dropping off from his peak year in 1961 and with rising star Boog Powell languishing in left field, first baseman Jim Gentile was traded to Kansas City for outfielder Norm Siebern.

Dramatically, the second "changing of the guard" in three years worked wonders for the Orioles, who reverted to their 1960–61 form. They had the best record in the American League over the two-year period of 1964–65, going a combined 191–133—but they still finished third both years.

TOP: Luis Aparicio was part of the long line of Orioles' outstanding shortstops, manning the position from 1963 to '67. He was elected to the Baseball Hall of Fame in 1984.

ABOVE: Hall of Fame executive Lee MacPhail was general manager and later president of the Orioles from 1958 until December 1965. Before leaving the club for a job in the commissioner's office, he put the pieces together for the trade that brought Frank Robinson to the Orioles.

" In 1964, Bauer's first year at the helm, Brooks Robinson had a career year (.317, 28 HRs, and 118 RBIs), which earned him MVP honors . . ."

In 1964, Bauer's first year at the helm, Brooks Robinson had a career year (.317, 28 HRs, and 118 RBIs), which earned him MVP honors; Boog Powell provided a huge presence with 39 homers and 99 RBIs; Norm Siebern contributed 106 walks and a .379 on-base percentage; rookie pitcher Wally Bunker posted a spectacular 19–5 record despite making only 29 starts; Milt Pappas recorded a 16–7 mark; and rejuvenated pitcher Robin Roberts (signed the year before after being released by the Phillies) went 13–7. The Orioles lowered the team's ERA to 3.16, and it all added up to a sparkling 97–65 record, but at season's end, it left them two games behind the Yankees and one game behind the White Sox.

The 1965 season proved to be tumultuous in the American League. The Orioles saw their team batting average fall 10 points to .238, with Brooks (.297) the only regular with an average higher than rookie Curt Blefary's .260 mark. That offensive slack, however, was more than offset by a pitching staff that had five starting pitchers (with a minimum of 24 games) with an ERA

OPPOSITE: Brooks Robinson—"Mr. Oriole"—was the American League's Most Valuable Player in 1964.
ABOVE LEFT: Mike McCormick was already a six-year veteran when the Orioles acquired him from the Giants at age twenty-four. He went 6–8 in 1963, then spent most of the '64 season in the minors before being dealt to the Senators.
ABOVE: Centerfielder Paul Blair won eight Gold Gloves in 13 seasons with the Orioles, 1964–1976.

OPPOSITE LEFT: First baseman Jim Gentile hit 124 homers and had 398 RBIs in four seasons with the Orioles (1960 to 1963). His best season came in 1961, when he batted .302 with 46 homers and tied Roger Maris for the AL lead with 146 RBIs.

OPPOSITE RIGHT: Wally Bunker won 19 games as a rookie in 1964 when he was named AL Rookie Pitcher of the Year.

OPPOSITE BOTTOM: Tigers' pitcher Denny McLain drops a sacrifice bunt as catcher Johnny Orsino rises and Brooks Robinson charges from third during the final game of the 1963 season.

BELOW: Wally Bunker relaxes in the dugout during the 1964 season. Bunker went 39–19 over three seasons from 1964 to 1966, but went only 5–7 the next two years before being the first pick of the expansion Kansas City Royals.

below 3.00, dropping the team ERA below that number for the first time with a club record 2.98.

It didn't affect the Orioles won-lost record or their third-place position, but the defending champion Yankees plunged to a surprising sixth place, while the Minnesota Twins claimed the American League title, and the White Sox finished second for the third straight year.

Blefary, who had 22 home runs and 70 RBIs to go with his .260 batting average, was named American League Rookie of the Year, and the Orioles had six pitchers win 10 or more games—Steve Barber (15–10), Stu Miller (14–7, plus 24 saves), Milt Pappas (13–9), Dick Hall (11–8), and Wally Bunker (10–8). Robin Roberts's record dropped to 5–7, leading to his release on July 31—but not before he served as a roommate and tutor for a raw rookie who would match Roberts's 1965 win total with a 5–4 record in his first season in the big leagues.

Jim Palmer had arrived, along with the dawn of a new era.

ABOVE: Left-hander Frank Bertaina spent parts of four seasons with the Orioles before being traded to the Senators in May 1967. His biggest game as an Oriole came in his fifth appearance, when he tossed a one-hitter to beat the Kansas City A's, 1-0.

RIGHT: Steve Barber pitches against the Red Sox in 1964. Barber became the Orioles' first 20-game winner in 1963 and won 95 games in eight seasons with the club.

PAGE 84: Jim Palmer enters in relief of Dave McNally on May 16, 1965, against the Yankees, his seventh major league appearance. He would go on to pitch 3 2/3 innings and earn the first of his 268 career victories.

PAGE 85: Rookie Jim Palmer crosses the plate after hitting his first home run on May 16, 1965, against the Yankees.

MEMORABLE GAMES
1961–1965

May 9, 1961

In a 13–5 win, Jim Gentile hits grand slams in the first and second innings at Minnesota's Metropolitan Stadium, becoming only the third major leaguer to hit two grand slams in a game and the first to do it in consecutive innings. He also had a sacrifice fly to set the club record with nine RBIs in a game.

August 30, 1961

In Paul Richards's final game as manager, the Orioles hit five home runs and Jack Fisher goes the distance despite walking a club record 12 batters in an 11–4 win over the Angels at Los Angeles' Wrigley Field. Jim Gentile, Jackie Brandt, Earl Robinson, Ron Hansen, and Jerry Adair go deep.

August 3, 1961

Hal "Skinny" Brown pitches his third straight shutout, beating Minnesota, 3–0, at Memorial Stadium, to run his scoreless stretch to a club-record 32 consecutive innings without allowing a run. His scoreless streak will go to 36 innings before he allows a lead-off home run in the fifth inning of his next start against Kansas City on August 8.

September 26, 1962

In his first major league start, Dave McNally beats the Kansas City Athletics, 3–0, in the shortest game ever played at Memorial Stadium—one hour and thirty-two minutes. It also is the big-league debut for Orioles catcher Andy Etchebarren.

May 26, 1963

Wes Stock becomes the only Orioles pitcher ever to win both games of a doubleheader as the Birds sweep the Indians in Cleveland. Stock enters in the fifth inning of the opener with the O's trailing 6–3 and leaves after working two perfect innings with the O's now ahead 7–6 in a 10–6 win. In the nightcap, Stock pitches the final three innings, allowing a hit and a walk as the Orioles break a 1–1 tie in the eighth and go on to win, 6–1.

May 5, 1964

In his first game of the season and second of his big-league career, nineteen-year-old rookie right-hander Wally Bunker tosses a one-hitter, beating Washington, 2–1. Chuck Hinton's fourth-inning single is the only hit allowed by Bunker, who will go on to win his first six games, toss another one-hitter, and win 19 games for the season to be named American League Rookie Pitcher of the Year.

September 18, 1963

After losing his previous two starts, Steve Barber becomes the first Oriole to win 20 games in a season, beating the Angels, 3–1, at Chavez Ravine with late-inning relief help from Dick Hall.

May 16, 1965

Nineteen-year-old rookie Jim Palmer enters in relief and wins his first major league game, beating New York, 7–5, at Memorial Stadium. Palmer also hits his first home run, a shot to right off the Yankees' Jim Bouton.

CHAPTER 5

FRANK ARRIVES

Before he cleaned off his desk in preparation for the 1965 Winter Meetings and his eventual move to New York, General Manager Lee MacPhail put together a couple of minor trades that caused little excitement and even less speculation. They did, however, pave the way for a spectacular sendoff for MacPhail, who left the Orioles at the end of November 1965 to take a position in the commissioner's office.

On December 2, veteran outfielder Norm Siebern, who had two mediocre years in Baltimore, was traded to the California Angels for Dick Simpson, a promising twenty-one-year-old prospect. Four days later Jackie Brandt, another veteran outfielder, and Darold Knowles, a young left-handed pitcher, were packaged to the Philadelphia Phillies in exchange for right-handed reliever Jack Baldschun.

Both trades made sense, since the Orioles had outfielders Paul Blair and Curt Blefary waiting in the wings, and they were in the market for a proven arm for the bullpen. But there was nothing to suggest these trades would lead to the bombshell announcement to follow. It would later be documented by both the outgoing and incoming general managers that MacPhail's last official act as GM of the Orioles was to give his successor Harry Dalton a piece of information, along with a piece of paper.

"You're the new GM," said MacPhail, breaking the news that owner Jerry Hoffberger had chosen Dalton to replace him, "and this is your first decision." The slip of paper contained four names for a proposed trade—right-hander Milt Pappas,

OPPOSITE: Frank Robinson turned the Orioles from a contending club into a winner immediately after being acquired from the Reds before the 1966 season, winning the AL Triple Crown that year.

the acknowledged ace of the O's young pitching staff, plus the recently acquired Baldschun and Simpson, who would be sent to the Cincinnati Reds in exchange for former National League MVP and Triple Crown winner Frank Robinson.

It turned out to be the easiest decision of Dalton's early tenure with the Orioles, which would be marked by both exhilaration and exasperation. The trade became a major turning point in the history of the franchise. "I just felt it was a deal that could put us over the top," Dalton recalled years later, "and that's how it turned out."

Frank's presence was noted early and often by teammates. "I think we just won the pennant," a wise twenty-year-old Jim Palmer famously said after watching the newcomer's first round of spring-training batting practice.

"Everything seemed to come together after Frank got here," said Brooks Robinson, the American League MVP in 1964 and the club's resident superstar at the age of only twenty-seven. "We were a good team already—but we just got better."

ABOVE: Traveling secretary Phil Itzoe checks the player ticket list before a game in Cleveland in 1966 while Curt Blefary and others sign team baseballs.
OPPOSITE TOP: The Orioles grounds crew tends the field in 1966.
OPPOSITE BOTTOM: Here come da Judge! Frank Robinson instituted a "kangaroo court" when he joined the Orioles in 1966, serving as judge and levying fines for boneheaded plays or silly comments after Orioles wins.

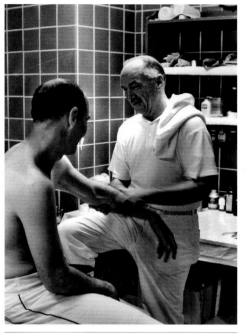

OPPOSITE: Dick Brown shared catching duties with John Orsino and Charlie Lau for three years after being acquired from the Tigers after the 1962 season. He reported to spring training in 1966 complaining of headaches, which later revealed the presence of a brain tumor, ending his career. He threw out the first pitch at the Orioles' first World Series home game that fall against the Dodgers and scouted for the team before passing away in 1970 at age thirty-five.
LEFT: Dick Hall, one of the top relief pitchers in Orioles history, stares in before delivering a pitch to Chicago's Moose Skowron during the 1966 season.
ABOVE: Eddie Weidner spent 46 years as the Orioles trainer, beginning with the International League Orioles in 1922.

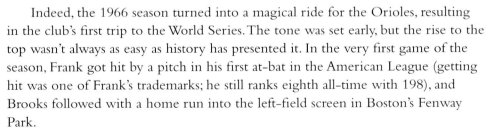

> **The 1966 season turned into a magical ride for the Orioles, resulting in the club's first trip to the World Series. The tone was set early, but the rise to the top wasn't always as easy as history has presented it.**

Indeed, the 1966 season turned into a magical ride for the Orioles, resulting in the club's first trip to the World Series. The tone was set early, but the rise to the top wasn't always as easy as history has presented it. In the very first game of the season, Frank got hit by a pitch in his first at-bat in the American League (getting hit was one of Frank's trademarks; he still ranks eighth all-time with 198), and Brooks followed with a home run into the left-field screen in Boston's Fenway Park.

Only a few weeks later, during a Mother's Day doubleheader, Frank struck the blow that would become the signature moment of his career in Baltimore—and one of the top moments in team history. The Cleveland Indians had arrived in town with a 14–1 record after opening the season with 10 straight wins.

The teams split the first two games of the four-game series. Then, in the opener of the doubleheader on May 8, Jim Palmer registered an 8–2 complete game win. The second game of the doubleheader would feature Cleveland's Luis Tiant and his spotless 3–0 record—three consecutive shutouts, a 27-inning scoreless streak, and an earned run average of 0.00. His first matchup against Frank Robinson would become the most memorable in Memorial Stadium history.

In the first inning, with one man on base and one out, Frank crushed a Tiant pitch. The high, arcing drive easily cleared the left-field wall, hooking and soaring

far enough to go over the grandstand seats. It was the only fair ball to leave the park in the Orioles' relatively young eleven-year history—and it remained as such for the thirty-eight-year history of Memorial Stadium.

The initial reaction to the home run was that it had shattered Tiant's scoreless streak and put the front-running Indians in their place, but the continuing buzz made it obvious that something special had happened. After a couple of minutes, it was determined that the ball had indeed left the park and witnesses, both inside and outside, approximated the landing spot—451 feet from home plate in the stadium parking lot. The subsequent announcement resulted in a celebration that few guessed would be a once-in-a-lifetime event.

It was the never-to-be-forgotten exclamation point on Frank Robinson's arrival in Baltimore. After that double-dip defeat, the Indians left Baltimore with the same 15–4 record as the Orioles. But after getting to 16–4, the Orioles lost four straight and 10 of the next 14 before things fell into place.

After that lackluster 19–14 start, the year's script took on a tone of finality. Frank, Brooks, and Boog Powell powered a drive that produced 47 wins in the next 65 games and a 66–32 record. The Orioles continued on cruise control leading up to September 22, 1966, when Palmer threw another complete game for a 6–1 win in Kansas City that clinched Baltimore's first pennant. That set up a 1966 World Series matchup against the heavily favored Los Angeles Dodgers, led by baseball's best pitching tandem, Sandy Koufax and Don Drysdale.

Then, in Game 1, the Robinsons hit back-to-back home runs in the first inning off Drysdale, and Moe Drabowsky came out of the bullpen to strike out 11, giving the Orioles a 5–2 victory, and the stage appeared set for an upset. In fact, the Dodgers would not score again after the third inning of that first game.

TOP: Orioles manager Hank Bauer confers with the umpires before the first World Series game ever played in Baltimore, Game 3 of the 1966 World Series at Memorial Stadium.
ABOVE: The Baltimore Symphony Orchestra entertains fans before the third game of the 1966 World Series.
RIGHT: Boog Powell rounds second during the 1966 World Series.
OPPOSITE TOP: Traffic on 33rd Street was one-way only for the 1966 World Series.
OPPOSITE BOTTOM: Brooks Robinson awaits the pitch . . . moves to his left . . . makes a difficult stop . . . throws to second . . . and gets the force during Game 3 of the 1966 World Series.
FOLLOWING PAGES: Curt Blefary at bat during the 1966 World Series.

In Game 2, Jim Palmer beat Koufax, 6–0, in what would prove to be the final game of Koufax's great career, and Wally Bunker and Dave McNally followed with 1-0 victories in an unprecedented sweep of the National League champions.

Fittingly, the year ended with Frank (who won the 1966 Triple Crown), Brooks, and Powell finishing first, second, and third in the voting for the American League Most Valuable Player Award. An Orioles' era that began with significant change both on and off the field and produced the organization's first World Series championship showed the team was well-positioned for a long run—but success doesn't come easily. As the Yankees had found out—dropping from first to last place in the period of two years—change in the standings could be drastic.

In 1967, almost overnight, or so it seemed, the Orioles' pitching staff was decimated by injuries. Palmer, the big winner in 1966 with a 15–10 record, would win only three games over the next two years, missing 1968 completely, because of injuries. Steve Barber, who finished 1966 on the disabled list, and Wally Bunker never regained the form that had seen them register careers highs of 20 and 19 wins, respectively, in 1963 and 1964.

McNally started only 22 games in 1967, compared to 33 the year before, leaving the Orioles with a makeshift rotation led by native Baltimorean Tom Phoebus, whose 14–9 record was easily the team's best. From a runaway 97–63 record in the magical championship run, the Orioles slid to a 76–85 record in 1967.

Over the two-year period following their World Series win, the Orioles saw their team batting average drop 33 points to .225, while run production fell off by 176 runs, down to 579. Those numbers were somewhat offset by an offensive decline throughout the league, but it was alarming nonetheless. While poor numbers are never a total accident, the Orioles could certainly partially attributable theirs to an accident on the basepaths, one that would have a lingering effect on Frank Robinson's career—and, no doubt, Manager Hank Bauer's long-range job security.

The accident took place on June 27, 1967, when Frank slid into second base intent on breaking up a double play. Frank's head hit the kneecap of White Sox second baseman Al Weis, and it was a week before Robinson found out he was safe on the play. Then, it would be almost two years before he would regain a semblance of the offensive form he displayed in 1966.

TOP: Paul Blair awaits Jim Lefebvre's eighth inning fly ball, then leaps to rob the Dodger infielder of a game-tying home run in Game 3 of the 1966 World Series. Blair's solo homer gave the Orioles a 1–0 victory.
OPPOSITE BOTTOM: American League president Joe Cronin looks on as Orioles broadcaster Chuck Thompson—working for NBC—interviews manager Hank Bauer after the 1966 World Series.
ABOVE: Acquired from the Senators in 1967, Pete Richert was the main lefty out of the bullpen for four-and-a-half years and pitched for three pennant-winning Orioles teams.

TOP: Brooks Robinson won 16 Gold Gloves in twenty-three years with the Orioles, more than any nonpitcher.

TOP RIGHT: Mike Adamson was a first-round pick of the Orioles in the secondary phase of the June 1967 draft, but he pitched in only 11 games over three seasons.

ABOVE: As a rookie reliever in 1966, Eddie Watt saved the Orioles by stepping into the rotation for 13 starts when injuries sidelined various starters. Over eight seasons with the O's, Watt excelled as the club's top reliever, appearing in 363 games with 74 saves and a 2.74 ERA.

RIGHT: Andy Etchebarren played in 12 seasons with the Orioles from 1962 to 1975. He made the AL All-Star team as a rookie catcher in 1966, when he set career highs in games, hits, doubles, homers, and RBIs.

OPPOSITE: "Mischievous Moe" Drabowsky not only set a record for a relief pitcher with 11 strikeouts in 6 2/3 innings in Game 1 of the 1966 World Series, but he made Commissioner Bowie Kuhn one of his legendary "hotfoot" victims in the clubhouse during the 1970 World Series.

When he was hurt in June, Frank was on the kind of pace that might've led to a repeat Triple Crown—he was hitting .337, with 21 home runs and 59 runs batted in. (Instead, Boston's Carl Yastrzemski became the second straight Triple Crown winner in 1967, with a .326 average, 44 HRs, 121 RBIs). Frank missed the next 33 games and hit only nine more homers, finishing the year at .311 with 30 home runs and 94 RBIs.

The Orioles, already struggling with a 32–36 record when Frank was injured, quickly went downhill from there. When the season ended, so too did the coaching careers of Sherm Lollar, Gene Woodling, and Harry Brecheen, a reprise of the exodus from Billy Hitchcock's staff after the 1962 season. Then, the Orioles promoted long-time minor league manager Earl Weaver to replace Woodling as the first-base coach, giving an early indication of the organization's future plans.

Through the 1968 season, Frank Robinson continued to struggle. He missed 32 more games and finished the season with career lows in home runs (15) and RBIs (52) while hitting just .258. As the club struggled, it became a matter of time before Dalton ushered in a complete changing of the guard. Manager Hank Bauer was fired during the All-Star break and replaced by Weaver. Also, George Staller joined third-base coach Bill Hunter, pitching coach George Bamberger, and bullpen coach Vern Hoscheit to give the Orioles a complete staff from the club's minor league system.

With a 43–37 record at the break, the change sparked an immediate six-game winning streak, and the Orioles went 48–34 the rest of the way to finish with a respectable 91–71 record. This wasn't even close to the runaway Tigers, but it still put them into position for a return to prominence.

BOTTOM: The winningest left-hander in club history, Dave McNally started Games 1 and 4 of the 1966 World Series, pitching a four-hit shutout in the last game as the Orioles swept the Dodgers in four straight. OPPOSITE: Here facing the Indians in 1968, Dave McNally had 181 victories in 13 seasons, ranking second only to Jim Palmer in club history. He won 20 or more games four straight years, 1968 through 1971.

MEMORABLE GAMES
1966-1968

June 21, 1966

With two on and two out in the ninth inning, right fielder Frank Robinson leaps to make a spectacular catch, falling onto the seats at Yankee Stadium and emerging with the ball to rob Roy White of a game-winning home run as the Orioles hold on to win, 7–5.

September 22, 1966

Russ Snyder makes a diving catch on a line drive to center field by the A's Dick Green for the final out, clinching the Orioles' first American League pennant. Jim Palmer posts a complete-game 6–1 victory at Kansas City's Municipal Stadium.

May 8, 1966

Frank Robinson hits a 451-foot home run off Cleveland's Luis Tiant, becoming the only player to hit a fair ball completely out of Memorial Stadium. The first-inning blast gives the O's a 2–0 lead on the way to an 8–3 win and a doubleheader sweep as the Orioles end Tiant's 27-inning scoreless streak and tie the Indians for first place. The Orioles place a flag on the back of the left field bleachers where Robinson's home run left the park, saying simply, "HERE."

October 5, 1966

In the team's first-ever World Series game, Brooks and Frank Robinson each homer in their first at bats and the Orioles go on to beat the Dodgers, 5–2, at Los Angeles.

April 30, 1967

Steve Barber and Stu Miller combine on a no-hitter but lose, 2–1, when Detroit scores twice in the ninth inning in the first game of a doubleheader at Memorial Stadium. In the game, Barber walks 10, hits two batters, and uncorks two wild pitches, the second tying the score in the ninth inning. Miller comes on with the bases loaded and one out and induces a potential double-play grounder, but Mark Belanger—who entered defensively at second base in the ninth inning—bobbles the throw from shortstop Luis Aparicio, allowing the go-ahead run to score.

April 27, 1968

On a wet Saturday afternoon at Memorial Stadium, right-hander Tom Phoebus tosses a no-hitter to beat Boston, 6–0. The Baltimore native fans nine, walks three, and retires the last 12 batters in order. Joe Foy strikes out to end the game, and catcher Curt Blefary—an outfielder making only his fourth start behind the plate—jubilantly gives the ball to Phoebus. The game, delayed one hour and twenty-three minutes by rain, draws 3,147 fans.

May 17, 1967

The Orioles hit a club-record seven home runs in a 12–8 win at Boston. Four of the homers (by Andy Etchebarren, Sam Bowens, Boog Powell, and Davey Johnson) come in a nine-run seventh inning. Paul Blair, Brooks Robinson, and Frank Robinson also go deep for the O's. The seven-homer game was matched on August 26, 1985, at California.

October 9, 1966

Dave McNally goes the distance in Game 4 as the Orioles sweep the heavily favored Dodgers to win their first World Series. The Birds blank LA over the final three games and win the last two at Memorial Stadium by 1–0 scores on home runs by Paul Blair (Game 3) and Frank Robinson (Game 4).

June 4, 1967

In the longest game in club history, Orioles pitchers set a club record by striking out 21 Washington Senators in a 19-inning, 7–5 win at Memorial Stadium. Five pitchers—Steve Barber (2 strikeouts), Wally Bunker (5), Eddie Watt (5), Eddie Fisher (3) and Stu Miller (6)—combine on the Ks, and the Orioles win on Andy Etchebarren's two-run homer in the 19th inning.

CHAPTER 6
THE BEST DAMN TEAM IN BASEBALL

T here was a definite feeling of resolve when the Orioles convened for Earl Weaver's first spring-training camp as a major league manager. The two disappointing seasons that followed the club's first World Series championship had left a sour taste, led to an overhaul of the staff, and raised questions about whether the O's were just another "one and done" wonder.

Before the 1969 season, doubts lingered about Frank Robinson and whether he would ever recover fully from his 1967 head injury. There was also some question about the depth of the pitching staff, which had lost starter Wally Bunker and reliever Moe Drabowsky in that year's expansion draft. Still, the second half of the 1968 season—in which Weaver compiled 48–34 record and led the team to 91–71 finish—left everyone with a feeling of optimism. Nobody could've predicted the level of dominance that would follow over the next three years, when the Orioles would proudly proclaim themselves "The Best Damn Team in Baseball," but the pieces were in place for an extended period of excellence.

"I remember going into spring training in 1969, that we had the feeling that we couldn't be beat," said first baseman Boog Powell. "We just had the feeling that if Frank did his thing, if Brooks did his thing, if I did my thing—nobody could stop us. One of the cool things was having [Don] Buford as the leadoff hitter all year. He really set the table for everybody. And with Brooks, Paulie [Blair], Mark [Belanger], and Davey [Johnson], nobody could touch our defense."

In fact, Powell proved to be the dominant offensive force as the Orioles powered to three straight American League pennants from 1969 through 1971. What really sparked the best run in team history, though, was the emergence of the best pitching staff in the American League, thanks in part to a relatively obscure

OPPOSITE: Younger fans may know him as the barbecue king of Eutaw Street, but for the better part of 14 seasons, Boog Powell was the sauce in the middle of the Orioles vaunted line up. He was the 1970 AL MVP, batting .297 with 35 homers and 114 RBIs—a year after finishing runner-up for the award with even better numbers (.304/37/121). After breaking into the lineup as a twenty-year-old in left field in 1962, Powell moved to first base full-time in 1966, and over the next nine years, anchored an infield that won 19 Gold Gloves—at every position but first. He hit 303 homers in 14 years with the Orioles, third on the club's list, and ranks among the top five in games, hits, RBIs, runs, walks, extra-base hits, and total bases.

FOLLOWING PAGES: Davey Johnson fields a grounder in Game 1 of the 1970 ALCS at Minnesota. Johnson won three Gold Gloves in seven seasons at second base for the Orioles from 1969 to 1971, and later he came back to manage the club to two postseason appearances.

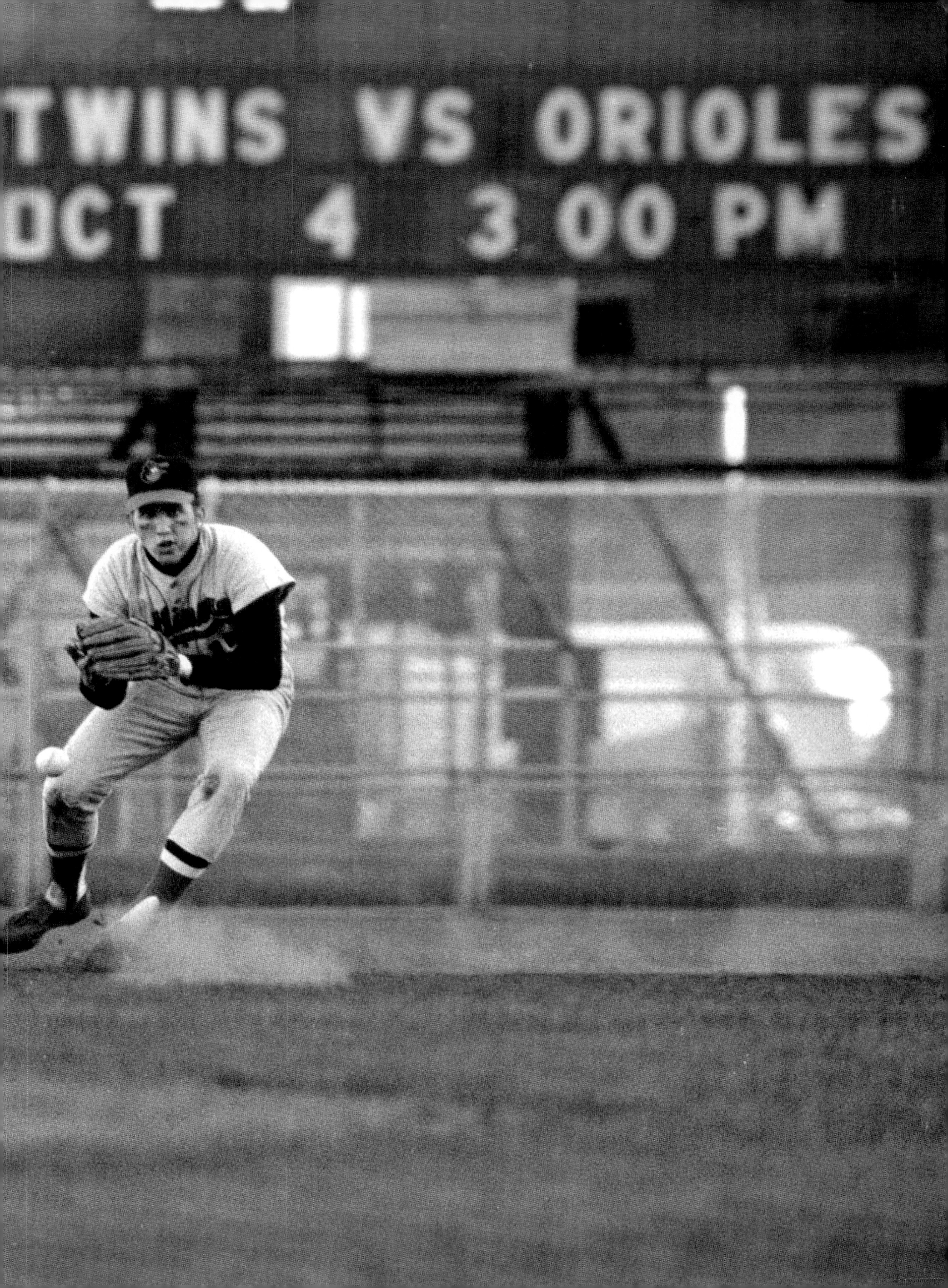
TWINS VS ORIOLES
OCT 4 3 00 PM

ABOVE: Don Buford was the Orioles left-fielder and lead-off hitter most of his five years with the Orioles and was the catalyst for three straight pennant-winning teams, scoring 99 runs in each of those seasons, between 1969 and 1971.
LEFT: From 1969 through 1975, Linda Warehime swept the bases—and, occasionally, visiting third base coaches—when the grounds crew dragged the field mid-game.
OPPOSITE: Brooks Robinson didn't like the long bill of the batting helmet, so he shaved it down.

off-season trade. Following the 1968 season, Curt Blefary, who had slumped badly after his Rookie of the Year season in 1966, was sent to Houston for left-hander Mike Cuellar, who, like his new team, had some previous success, but he was relatively unheralded coming out of the National League. It would prove to be one of the best trades ever made.

All Cuellar did was reach the 20-win mark three straight years, for 67 wins total and a share of the Cy Young Award in 1969. In addition, the Orioles caught a break when Jim Palmer was passed over in the same expansion draft that claimed Bunker and Drabowsky. Any further questions about pitchers were quickly dismissed.

After missing all but a handful of games the previous two years, Palmer rebounded in 1969 with a vengeance. Despite making only 23 starts, he posted a 16–4 record to go with a 2.34 earned run average—and he did so as the rotation's fourth starter, working behind Baltimore native Tom Phoebus (14–7). The only downside to an otherwise spectacular regular season was that the Orioles lost five in a row (their longest losing streak of the year) in the last week to finish 109–53.

This was two games shy of the American League's single-season record of 111 wins, set by the Cleveland Indians. Any sense of a letdown, however, was forgotten when the AL East champion Orioles swept the AL West champion Minnesota Twins in the newly created League Championship Series, as the majors for the first time divided their leagues into two divisions.

After beating the Twins in three straight in the American League Championship Series (ALCS), the Orioles returned to the World Series for the second time, where they were prohibitive favorites over the "Miracle Mets," a perennial loser who came out of nowhere to win the National League East and then beat the Braves in the NLCS that year.

Don Buford led off the first game of the World Series with a home run and the Orioles won, 4–1, but that would be the lone highlight for Baltimore. The underdog New York Mets won the next four games in what still is regarded as perhaps the biggest upset in World Series history.

"Our pitching was so good we felt we were unbeatable, which is why that season still stings," said Boog Powell. "I don't think we took them lightly; we knew they could play. I think the only guy who really surprised us was [Gary] Gentry— we didn't realize he threw that hard—but we knew about the rest of them. I still think if we'd played them 100 times, we'd win 80, but they made so many plays, and you have to give them credit. They didn't make any mistakes."

If there had been a feeling of resolve when the 1969 season started, the way it ended left the Orioles with a sense of urgency. They remained convinced they were the best team in baseball, and that air of invincibility didn't diminish, but the Orioles did acknowledge they had unfinished business.

Buoyed by Jim Palmer's resurgence the year before, and with Mike Cuellar fitting into the top of the rotation alongside Dave McNally, who was coming off back-to-back 20-win seasons, pitching coach George Bamberger boldly predicted that the Orioles would have three 20-game winners in 1970. The mission was accomplished

OPPOSITE: In three seasons with the Orioles, from 1969 to 1971, catcher Clay Dalrymple played in only 73 games, partly because of a broken ankle suffered in a home plate collision during the 1970 season. He went 2-for-2 as a pinch-hitter in the 1969 World Series, with hits off Nolan Ryan and Tom Seaver.
ABOVE: Jay Mazzone, who lost both hands in a fire when he was two years old, served as visiting team batboy in 1966 before becoming the Orioles batboy for the next five years. He worked four World Series and was the American League team's batboy for the 1966 All-Star Game in St. Louis.
FOLLOWING PAGES: Frank Robinson rounds third in Game 3 of the 1970 World Series.

that season with relative ease, when Palmer (20–10) reached the milestone in his 35th start on September 20, joining McNally (24–9) and Cuellar (24–8).

That year, Powell, who had been runner-up to Harmon Killebrew for Most Valuable Player in 1969, emerged as the leader of the offense. The slugging first baseman followed up his 1969 season (.304 average, 37 HRs, 121 RBIs) with a second straight monster performance, hitting 35 home runs, driving in 114 runs, and compiling a .297 batting average—and moved up a notch by winning the 1970 American League MVP Award. While Frank Robinson missed 30 games, Brooks Robinson did his part (18 HRs, 98 RBIs), and Merv Rettenmund burst onto the scene with a .322 average, 18 home runs, and 58 runs batted in, despite limited playing time. Meanwhile, Paul Blair (18 HRs, 65 RBIs) and Don Buford (17 HRs, 66 RBIs) helped make the defense as spectacular as ever.

As they had in 1969, the Orioles quickly took command of the American League's Eastern Division race, taking the lead for good on April 26 and finishing 15 games ahead of the Yankees. The Orioles' 108–54 record missed their previous

BELOW LEFT: Orioles manager Earl Weaver and Twins manager Bill Rigney pose before the 1970 ALCS opener at Minnesota. The Orioles went on to sweep the Twins for the second straight year.
BELOW RIGHT: Brooks Robinson robs Johnny Bench of a hit during the 1970 World Series.
OPPOSITE TOP LEFT: Jim Palmer shows the classic form that made him a first-ballot Hall of Fame selection in 1990.
OPPOSITE TOP RIGHT: Dave McNally (front) and Andy Etchebarren head to the clubhouse after the Orioles beat the Twins, 11–3, in the second game of the ALCS at Minnesota, October 4, 1970.
FOLLOWING PAGES: The Orioles celebrate their second World Championship in 1970.

year's mark by one game. There was, however, a noticeable difference in how the season ended.

The Orioles rolled into the playoffs with a 10-game winning streak, and they swept the Twins in three games in the first round of the playoffs for the second year in a row. This set up a classic powerhouse duel with the Cincinnati Reds in the 1970 World Series.

After earning one-run wins in the first two games, the Orioles thumped the Reds, 9–3, in Game 4, highlighted by a grand slam by pitcher Dave McNally, whose complete game victory gave his team a commanding 3–0 lead in the series. Despite giving up a late lead and losing Game 4, the Orioles came back with another 9–3 victory in Game 5 to win the series.

Paul Blair batted .474 for the series, but was overshadowed by the fielding wizardry of Brooks Robinson, who also hit .429 with two homers and a team-high six RBIs. The Orioles outhomered the Reds, 10–5, and outscored them, 32–20.

"I guess 'The Big Red Machine' got clogged up with Bird seed," quipped Boog Powell, when asked to sum up the series.

While the 1970 World Series ended up being a personal showcase for Brooks Robinson, it didn't start that way: Brooks made an error on his very first chance in the first game. "It was the simplest little two-hopper you could imagine," he recalled later. "After I messed it up, all I could think about was the previous year against the Mets—'Uh, oh here we go again.' Fortunately, things got better after that."

In fact, Robinson turned in a highlight reel of fielding gems, leading the Reds manager Sparky Anderson to say, "He can throw his glove out there and it will start double plays by itself."

Pete Rose said simply, "Brooks Robinson belongs in a higher league."

OPPOSITE TOP: Mark Belanger steps in to lead off the first game of the 1970 ALCS at Minnesota.
OPPOSITE BOTTOM: Before Game 3 of the 1970 ALCS, all signs pointed to the Orioles sweeping the Twins for the second straight year . . . and they did!
ABOVE: Elrod Hendricks (left) congratulates Dick Hall after the pitcher tossed 4 2/3 innings of one-hit relief to earn the win in Game 1 of the 1970 ALCS at Minnesota.

LEFT: World Series MVP Brooks Robinson and Game 5 winning pitcher Mike Cuellar celebrate the Orioles' second World Championship in 1970.
OPPOSITE: (top) Fans and players celebrate after winning the 1970 World Series against the Reds; (middle left) Orioles owner Jerry Hoffberger gets a whirlpool bath from (left to right) Pete Richert, Frank Robinson, and Davey Johnson after the Orioles win the 1970 World Series; (middle right) Elrod Hendricks leads the cheers after the Orioles win the 1970 World Series; (bottom) Don Buford and Pete Richert hoist the 1970 World Series trophy surrounded by George Staller, Clay Dalrymple, George Bamberger, equipment manager Clay Reid, Bill Hunter, Tom Phoebus, Moe Drabowsky, Terry Crowley, and Chico Salmon.

In 1971, things continued to go right for the Orioles, leaving little doubt about their clear superiority over the rest of the American League. The Orioles didn't stand pat after their World Series victory over the Reds, and during the off-season they engineered a trade that sent Phoebus, who shared the number-four spot in the rotation with Jim Hardin in 1970, to the San Diego Padres in exchange for Pat Dobson, a right-hander who had impressed in an earlier stint with the Detroit Tigers.

Assessing his starting rotation during spring training in 1971, Bamberger went out on a limb again, this time predicting that the addition of Dobson would give the Orioles four 20-game winners. Even though it developed a little slower and the club wasn't quite as dominant, the season went much like the previous two.

Although he again missed significant time in what would prove to be his final year in Baltimore, Frank Robinson put together another solid season, hitting .281, with 28 homers and 99 RBIs, while Brooks Robinson continued his consistent streak, posting a .272 average, 20 homers, and 92 RBIs. Powell missed 30 games and saw his average dip to .256, but he still produced 22 home runs and 92 RBIs. Meanwhile, Merv Rettenmund continued his progress, hitting .318 and driving in 75 runs.

The Orioles were also developing budding stars in the minors, and some were close to being ready for the majors, but for now the Orioles plowed ahead with the team they had, again finishing the season with a 10-game win streak and a 101–57 record, putting them in first place, 12 games ahead of the second-place Tigers. Ultimately, on September 26, 1971, Jim Palmer again made good on Bamberger's

boast. Making his 37th and final start of the year, Palmer became the Orioles' fourth pitcher to reach the 20-win plateau, something that hadn't happened since the 1920 Chicago White Sox. What made the feat even more remarkable was the fact that Dave McNally, who led the staff with a 21–4 record, made only 30 starts. Palmer and Mike Cuellar both finished with 20–9 records, while Pat Dobson was 20–8.

In the playoffs, the Orioles again swept the best-of-five ALCS, this one 3–0 over Oakland. This ran their ALCS win streak to nine and set up a very classic Fall Classic, with the Orioles facing the Pittsburgh Pirates in the 1971 World Series.

Unfortunately, this series ended in disappointment, though it wasn't the startling upset they experienced against the Mets in 1969. Simply put, the Orioles offense succumbed to the Pirates suddenly-powerful pitching staff. After prevailing in the first two games, the Orioles lost the next three: the Pirates' Steve Blass allowed one run in a complete-game victory, Bruce Kison allowed only one hit in six scoreless innings to stymie the Orioles' offense (in the first night game in World Series history), and Nelson Briles threw a two-hit shutout.

Dave McNally and the Orioles prevailed in Game 6, sending this exceptionally exciting series to Game 7—which ended in a 2–1 loss, a majestic pitching duel

TOP LEFT: Despite pitching in only three games for the Orioles in 1959 and 10 in his big league career, George Bamberger became the epitome of pitching coaches in ten years with the Orioles, from 1968 to 1977.
TOP RIGHT: Lefty reliever Pete Richert is interviewed by broadcasters Chuck Thompson and Tony Kubek after the 1970 World Series.
ABOVE: After winning Minor League Player of the Year honors in 1968 at AAA Rochester, outfielder Merv Rettenmund joined the Orioles in September that year, and over the next five seasons, played on four Eastern Division champs and three AL pennant winners. He led the Orioles twice in batting—.322 in 1970 and .318 in 1971—before being traded to the Reds after the 1973 season.
OPPOSITE: Pat Dobson gets congratulations from catcher Clay Dalrymple after striking out 13 A's in a 1–0 win over Catfish Hunter on July 11, 1971.

BROOKS ROBINSON: MR. ORIOLE

Brooks Robinson was among the first to be tested by the revolving-door policy that was in place throughout the 1950s. The fact that he outlasted everyone, including those who put it in place, and went on to become the face of the franchise is enough to suggest that Brooks Robinson was Paul Richards's most enduring Oriole legacy.

It was Richards, operating as manager-general manager, who convinced Brooks that Baltimore was his best bet for a quick ascent to the big leagues. Richards offered the teenage Brooks a Class B, instead of Class D, minor league assignment, which was the difference between the future Hall of Famer joining the Orioles and not the Detroit Tigers.

"A lot of people thought I was going to sign with Detroit because I was working out with the Little Rock Travelers, a Tigers' farm team," said Robinson. "But they were going to send me to Panama City, their Class D club, and Richards said the Orioles would send me to York, Pennsylvania. He promised the Orioles would give me the best chance, and they did."

In York, Robinson made the shift from second to third base. Brooks said it was George Staller, his manager at York, who suggested the move. He said, "I guess I didn't have a lot of range at second, but it was no big deal. If you can catch the ball, you can catch the ball." And Brooks hit enough to earn a promotion to the big leagues at the tender age of eighteen.

Brooks's debut, on September 17, 1955, gave the appearance of a smashing success. "I got two hits in my first game and might have gotten the wrong idea the big leagues wouldn't be that tough," Robinson recalled. "But then I went 0-for-18 and struck out 10 times and reality set in.

"I never had the feeling that I wasn't going to make it, but it was a learning process. In retrospect I'm glad I had those years in the minor leagues. At that age you're just not ready to play in the big leagues. I'm glad I had the chance to learn in the minor leagues."

He appeared in the major leagues every year from 1955 until his retirement in 1977, but he started slow. After playing some at Class AA in 1956 and AAA in 1957, Brooks spent the entire 1958 season in Baltimore, but his major league journey wasn't quite complete. "I was in the big leagues the whole year but didn't quite distinguish myself," Brooks said. "I had spent six months in the service before the '59 season, so I was a little behind when the season started."

In 1959, Richards took Brooks to lunch shortly before the player's twenty-second birthday, and Brooks wasn't quite prepared for what Richards said. "He told me he was sending me to Vancouver to play every day and that he would bring me back after the All-Star Game. But you never know how that's going to work out, you could go out there and they'd forget about you, but Paul kept his word," said Robinson.

Even then, success didn't come overnight. In fact, it took another month. Brooks would finish the 1959 season with a .284 average, but counting his 4-for-20 start, he went 17-for-95 and didn't get over .200 for good until August 14, 1959. From that point, however, he hit a blistering .346, and with his magical glove work on full display, Robinson was on his way. "I was just a better player when I came back from Vancouver," he explained.

"Things seemed to come together for me and the team in 1960 [when he finished third in the MVP voting], then 1964 was kind of a breakthrough year for me, and then came the turnaround in 1966, when we won for the first time. That was a special time, and after a little down spell we went on a good roll a few years later."

In the midst of the Orioles' three straight pennant-winning runs, the 1970 World Series became the signature event of Robinson's career. He already had league (1964) and All-Star (1966) MVP Awards, and he added a World Series MVP in 1970. Brooks was so dominant, the award was almost anticlimactic, and his defensive play inspired his most famous nickname, one that was fifteen years in the making. "Where do they plug Mr. Hoover in?" asked Cincinnati first baseman and future teammate Lee May, who, mesmerized by Brooks's defensive genius, coined the phrase the "Human Vacuum Cleaner."

Brooks Robinson was the team's first "signature" signee; the first prodigy to reach the major leagues; the player who turned out to be the best and lasted the longest; the one who wore the tag "face of the franchise" for most of the team's six-decade history. Quite a run for the guy who worked his way through that revolving door; who made Gold Glove awards a standard of Orioles' excellence; who became part of a community that embraced him as a twenty-year-old and never let go.

So, how does all that feel in retrospect? "It feels wonderful . . . to play my whole career in Baltimore is a great feeling. I feel like I had a great rapport with the fans. As I said [at the unveiling of his statue at Camden Yards in 2012], 'I don't consider them my fans, I consider them my friends.'"

And they consider him their legend.

between complete-game winner Steve Blass and the Orioles' Mike Cuellar. That game not only handed the Orioles their second disappointing World Series setback in three years, but it signaled the end of an era, bringing to a close one of the most dominant three-year runs in baseball history.

Was it also one of the best teams of all time? Some have made that case. During that stretch, the club compiled a 318–164 (.660) record; pitchers McNally, Cuellar, Palmer, and Dobson got 20 wins an astounding nine times collectively; Brooks Robinson, Mark Belanger, Paul Blair, and Davey Johnson won eleven Gold Gloves; Boog Powell hit 94 home runs and drove in 327 runs; and Don Buford score 99 runs each year, leading the league in 1971.

It was truly a remarkable run, one that probably fell one World Series win short of all-time status, but still a magnificent period of excellence. "I think if we had won that World Series against the Mets, we'd have been ranked among the game's best teams, but it didn't happen," said Brooks Robinson.

"My opinion of that team hasn't changed," added Powell. "We were a dynasty; I don't care what anybody says. We were a damn good team."

Or, as *Sports Illustrated* called the Orioles in a 1971 cover story, "The Best Damn Team in Baseball."

MEMORABLE GAMES
1969-1971

October 6, 1969

The Orioles thrash the Twins, 11–2, at Minnesota to sweep the three-game series and advance to the World Series for the second time in team history.

August 13, 1969

In his second start back after spending nearly six weeks on the disabled list, Jim Palmer tosses an 8–0 no-hitter against the Oakland A's at Memorial Stadium, walking six with eight strikeouts.

October 5, 1970

The Orioles beat the Twins, 6–1, to sweep Minnesota in the ALCS for the second straight year. Jim Palmer tosses a complete game, and Davey Johnson hits his second homer of the series, keying the win at Memorial Stadium.

October 4, 1969

In the first-ever American League Championship Series game, Paul Blair's two-out bunt in the 12th inning scores Mark Belanger to give the Eastern Division champion Orioles a 4–3 win over Western Division champ Minnesota at Memorial Stadium.

October 9, 1969

Don Buford becomes the first player to lead off a World Series Game 1 with a home run, and the Orioles beat the Mets, 4–1, in Game 1. The Mets, however, come back to win the next four games to take the title.

October 15, 1970

Mike Cuellar goes the distance and the Orioles beat the Reds, 9–3, to capture their second World Series title. Fittingly, the final out comes on a ground ball to third baseman Brooks Robinson, whose superb fielding exploits, .429 batting average, and two home runs during the series earn him MVP honors.

September 21, 1971

Dave McNally shuts out New York, 5–0, at Yankee Stadium, his fourth straight season with 20 or more wins. He is the first of four Orioles who will win 20 games in 1971. Mike Cuellar and Pat Dobson join him on September 24 and Jim Palmer on September 26, as the Orioles join the 1920 White Sox as the only teams with four 20-game winners.

September 13, 1971

After homering in the Orioles' 9–1 win in the first game of a doubleheader, Frank Robinson goes deep with two outs in the ninth inning off Detroit's Fred Scherman for his 500th career homer. Frank becomes the eleventh player in big league history to reach 500 home runs.

October 5, 1971

New opponent, same results: The Orioles sweep the A's in the ALCS for their third straight trip to the World Series.

October 17, 1971

After taking a 2–0 lead in the World Series, the Orioles drop four of the last five games to the Pirates and lose the series. In Game 7, Steve Blass outpitches Mike Cuellar, and the Orioles lose, 2–1.

CHAPTER 7
TIMING IS EVERYTHING

W ho could've seen all this coming? During the five-year period from 1972 to 1976, General Manager Harry Dalton left, Frank Robinson went with the trade winds, a work stoppage produced an uneven schedule, the DH arrived in the American League, the Orioles won two more division titles, the team did and did not go up for sale, and superstar Reggie Jackson showed up . . . just in time for free agency.

After running off three straight American League pennants, the Orioles experienced what arguably could be described as the most tumultuous decade in franchise history.

Prior to the 1972 season, it became obvious that on-field changes were imminent. The Orioles' minor league department had been recognized as the best in baseball for the better part of two decades and moves were inevitable: players like Don Baylor and Bobby Grich were waiting for promotion, and Merv Rettenmund, who had bounced back and forth between the majors and minors, needed more playing time at the major league level.

Changes occurred in the front office as well. Shortly after the 1971 World Series, Harry Dalton—the team's general manager who had been instrumental in the success of the minor league department—accepted an offer to take over as president and general manager of the California Angels.

Orioles' team president Frank Cashen assumed Dalton's duties and promoted Don Pries from the minor league staff to be assistant general manager. Pries would

OPPOSITE: Acquired in a 1976 trade with the Yankees that also brought Tippy Martinez and Rick Dempsey to the Orioles, left-hander Scott McGregor was a staple of the rotation for more than a decade. He won 20 games in 1980, was named to the AL All-Star team in 1981, and pitched complete game shutouts to clinch the 1979 AL Championship Series as well as the 1983 World Series.

help guide the team through an extended transition period. In a touch of irony, the first order of business was to arrange a trade of Frank Robinson, whose acquisition six years earlier had been credited with jump-starting the Orioles' period of American League dominance.

Don Baylor had been the Minor League Player of the Year in 1970, when he hit .327, with 22 home runs and 107 RBIs for AAA Rochester; he backed it up in 1971 by hitting .313, with 20 home runs and 95 RBIs. Baylor's big-league promotion in 1972 was the key for the Orioles when they traded Frank to the Dodgers for pitcher Doyle Alexander. In recognition of Frank's contributions to the club, the Orioles consulted with him in advance and guaranteed his wish to be traded, if necessary, to a West Coast team, a noble gesture, but one that restricted their bargaining power.

The timing, as it turned out, couldn't have been worse. In 1973, one year later, the American League adopted the designated hitter rule. The league did this because they were alarmed by a sudden downturn in offense, which was demonstrated by the 1972 Orioles more than any other team. Since Robinson continued to be reasonably productive over the next four years, three of them primarily as a designated hitter, the Orioles would no doubt have benefited by keeping him.

Undoubtedly, losing Robinson in 1972 had a negative effect on the entire Orioles' lineup, but the team felt they could weather it. After all, the Orioles were coming off a 101–57 season that saw them score 742 runs, with a pitching staff that compiled a stingy 2.99 earned run average. They had also experienced three straight 100-plus win seasons, something that had been done only twice before in American League history.

OPPOSITE: No one spent more time in an Orioles uniform than Elrod Hendricks. He played all or part of 11 seasons in three different stints with the Orioles, platooning at catcher, before serving twenty-eight years as the club's bullpen coach.

ABOVE: Roric Harrison spent the first of his five big league seasons with the Orioles, pitching in relief in 1972. He would be the last AL pitcher to homer—on the final day of the '72 season at Cleveland—before the league adopted the designated hitter rule the following season, and he was the last Oriole pitcher to homer until Kris Benson did so at Shea Stadium against the Mets during interleague play in 2006.

RIGHT: Tommy Davis was acquired from the Cubs in August 1972 after a long career spent mostly as an outfielder in the National League. But with the introduction of the designated hitter in 1973, Davis became the Orioles' primary DH for three years, batting .306, .289, and .283 and driving in more than 80 runs twice.

EARL WEAVER:
THE EARL OF BALTIMORE

PROFILE

Whenever he reflected on his Hall of Fame career with the Orioles, Earl Weaver said there were two aspects that never ceased to amaze him—the unlikely path he took to the big leagues and the never-ending affection of Baltimore fans.

"How does it happen that a person who tried for ten years as a player and another ten as a manager [all in the minor leagues], someone who was just happy to be in baseball, ever reach the major leagues?" Weaver asked during his induction speech in Cooperstown on August 4, 1996. "It took a lot of guts by a lot of people who were not afraid to give an unknown a chance—Harry Dalton, who was the general manager, had to convince Frank Cashen, who was the president, who had to convince owner Jerry Hoffberger, that I was ready to do the job.

"It must have taken a lot of courage for them to turn a major league team over to someone like me, and if they knew how nervous I was, they might have had some second thoughts," said Weaver, who at thirty-eight became the youngest manager in the big leagues when he succeeded Hank Bauer in 1968. "Fortunately, I feel like I justified their confidence."

Weaver, who had a winning record as a manager in each of his last 10 minor league seasons, joined the Orioles under awkward circumstances before that 1968 season. He was named first-base coach when Bauer's staff was almost completely dismantled, with third-base coach Bill Hunter the sole surviving member. Although he was perceived by many as the "manager in waiting," Weaver always insisted his dream of reaching the big leagues had been satisfied when he was named coach.

"Once I got there, all I ever wanted was to do a good enough job to stay in the big leagues long enough to earn a pension," Weaver often said, noting that it took four years at that time to qualify. Instead, he stayed long enough—seventeen seasons over two stretches—to compile a 1,480–1,060 (.583 pct.) record, earn a plaque in Cooperstown, a statue at Oriole Park at Camden Yards, and a prominent place in Baltimore baseball lore.

Bill Hunter was himself considered a prime candidate to succeed Bauer in 1968, and he became a trusted friend and ally on what Weaver called "one of the greatest coaching staffs ever put together." In addition to Hunter, coaches Frank Robinson, George Bamberger, Jim Frey, Ray Miller, and Cal Ripken Sr. all went on to become major league managers. Coach Elrod Hendricks spent more time in an Orioles' uniform than anyone in club history, while George Staller, Jimmy Williams, Ralph Rowe, and Ken Rowe all traveled the same minor league path as Weaver.

"I was lucky enough to have six players who are in the Hall of Fame—Brooks and Frank Robinson, Jim Palmer, Reggie Jackson, Eddie Murray, and Cal Ripken Jr.—and when you have players like that, it's easy to manage," said Weaver, who admitted to special delight in breaking in Murray and Ripken as rookies. "But I also owe thanks to every player who ever put on a uniform for me. The players deserve the credit. I put their name in the lineup, but that didn't win games. What they did on the field won games. I was just the guy lucky enough to put their names in the lineup."

Weaver had more than his share of thrills during his triumphant ride with the Orioles, but perhaps none touched him more than having his statue included in the picnic area of Oriole Park—and the fact that he was able to attend all six of the statue unveilings in 2012. The timing was fortunate, for Weaver died only a few months later, on January 19, 2013.

"It's amazing how many people remember you," he said shortly after his ceremony. "It's been twenty-six years [since he had managed the Orioles]—and they still remember you. Throughout the years, the fans have been great. They couldn't have been better—and some of them weren't even around. They had to read a lot of books.

"And now, to look at this [his statue] and realize that you'll be remembered forever is an unbelievable feeling. Mr. [Peter] Angelos didn't have to do this. It's like a dream, and I'm very grateful. My wish now is to come back and watch Buck [Showalter] manage in playoff games and the World Series. I thank Mr. Angelos and I thank [sculptor] Toby Mendez, who made me look like Buck."

Earl didn't get his wish, but his words clearly indicated he was delighted to pass the torch, signaling the dawn of another successful era.

ABOVE: Earl Weaver always seemed to be yelling at someone during his more than fourteen years as Orioles manager.
OPPOSITE: Earl Weaver's statue at Camden Yards is framed by fireworks.

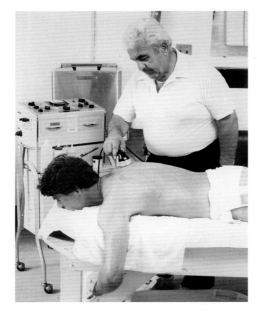

Further, the 1972 pitching staff lopped nearly half a run per game off the team's ERA, to a team record 2.53. Given this, the loss of Robinson should've been little more than a bump in the road enroute to a fourth straight pennant. The first players' strike in baseball history struck a dozen or so games from the calendar in April, but still: only four pitchers (Jim Palmer, Mike Cuellar, Dave McNally, and Pat Dobson), all with ERAs 2.95 or lower, started 143 of the season's 154 games. Manager Earl Weaver would use only 11 pitchers total the entire season—by way of contrast, thirty-one years later, a total of 14 *starting pitchers* would be utilized by Manager Buck Showalter.

But superb pitching in 1972 wasn't enough to overcome their offensive woes. The team's total runs scored dropped by an incredible 223 runs (from 742 to 519), which sent the Orioles' spiraling to an 80–74 record. No regular had a higher batting average than the .278 mark posted by Bobby Grich, who also led the club with a mere 66 runs scored. No one had more home runs or runs batted in than Boog Powell's modest totals of 21 and 81. The loss of Frank Robinson, the man credited with being the catalyst to the team's successful six-year run, was clearly critical.

No other team suffered such an alarming drop in production, and American League teams suffered a worse downward trend in comparison to National League teams. As a result, American League owners adopted the designated hitter rule following the '72 season. In response, the Orioles engineered a series of off-season trades as part of a major makeover to try to cure their power deficiency.

Their first such move was hardly a rousing success, even though the Orioles did experience a dramatic offensive turnaround in 1973. Pat Dobson, a two-year mainstay in the starting rotation, and second baseman Davey Johnson, were the principal players in a deal that brought catcher Earl Williams from Atlanta, where he had been one of the National League's top home run threats.

TOP: Ralph Salvon (here working on Jim Palmer) spent twenty-three years with the Orioles, including twenty years, from 1968 to '87, as head trainer.
ABOVE: To satisfy manager Earl Weaver's quest for a power-hitting catcher after missing the playoffs in 1972, the Orioles acquired Earl Williams from the Braves in exchange for four players. But after leading the club with 22 homers and driving in 83 runs in his first season, Williams slid to 14 homers and 52 RBIs in 1974 and battled with Weaver over his ambivalence toward catching. Though the Orioles won the AL East in '73 and '74, Williams was traded back to the Braves with cash for a minor league pitcher.
RIGHT: Andy Etchebarren (left) is congratulated by Brooks Robinson after his three-run homer in the seventh inning of Game 4 of the 1973 ALCS at Oakland. The O's won the game but lost the decisive Game 5, and the series, the next day.

But the dimensions at Memorial Stadium weren't as friendly for Williams as those he enjoyed in Atlanta, even though his 22 home runs led the club and his 83 runs batted in were second to the 89 posted by Tommy Davis, who emerged as the team's primary designated hitter (after Terry Crowley opened the season as DH). Despite paltry power numbers, the Orioles' enjoyed a resounding offensive resurgence thanks in large part to rookie outfielders Al Bumbry and Rich Coggins, who occupied the top two spots in the lineup.

Bumbry's .337 average, including a league-leading 11 triples, earned him Rookie of the Year honors. Playing an almost identical platoon role as Bumbry (both played 110 games), Coggins was an effective counterpart, hitting .319. In similar roles, Rettenmund and Baylor combined for 20 homers and 95 RBIs as the Orioles increased their run production a staggering 235 runs (519 to 754). The advent of the DH obviously played a role as Tommy Davis finished with a .306 average. However, the Orioles' wildly erratic run production totals over these three seasons remains today one of the team's great mysteries.

Meanwhile, the Orioles' pitching staff, even with an ERA that spiked to 3.07, for the most part remained a mystery to the rest of the American League,

ABOVE: Al Bumbry spent 13 seasons as an Orioles outfielder, winning AL Rookie of the Year honors in 1973 and becoming the first player in club history to amass 200 hits in a season.

ABOVE: One of the most popular players to put on an Orioles uniform, Al Bumbry moved from left field to center, made the AL All-Star team in 1980, and became a staple in the lineup for more than 12 seasons. Bumbry also won a bronze star as a platoon leader in Vietnam.

"*Despite paltry power numbers, the Orioles' enjoyed a resounding offensive resurgence thanks in large part to rookie outfielders Al Bumbry and Rich Coggins, who occupied the top two spots in the lineup.*"

ABOVE: Bobby Grich (left) and Mark Belanger gave the Orioles a Gold Glove double-play combination at second base and shortstop from 1973 through 1976.

with Palmer showing the way with a 22–9 record and 2.40 ERA. The result was yet another amazing turnaround in the win column. The Orioles finished with a 97–65 mark, which was good enough to dominate the AL East—but the team lost in the ALCS to the Oakland A's, who were in the process of winning the second of three straight World Series championships.

After the 1973 season, the O's were once again active in the off-season trade market, sending Rettenmund to Cincinnati in exchange for left-handed pitcher Ross Grimsley, leading Reds' manager Sparky Anderson to make what turned out to be an accurate prediction. "Ross will throw a lot of changeups and use up all of the ground in center field, and win you about 15 games," Anderson told Frank Cashen after the deal was made. Grimsley would go on to win 36 games in three years, 18 of them in his first year, 1974.

With the roster in a more settled state, the Orioles appeared to be in position for another run of dominance, but there were signs of unrest. With attendance fluctuating around the one million mark, there was speculation that owner Jerry Hoffberger was looking to sell the team. Hoffberger initially denied these rumors through the mid-1970s, until it became obvious it was a question of when, not if, ownership would change hands.

In the meantime, the 1974 season was marked by disappointment: the experiment with Earl Williams wasn't working out; Al Bumbry and Rich Coggins suffered through miserable second seasons; Boog Powell was on the verge of being phased out of first base in favor of Williams and Enos Cabell; and Brooks Robinson showed signs of decline. Run production took another significant drop (to 659). On top of that Jim Palmer, the rock of the rotation, suffered through an injury-riddled year, finishing 7–12.

ABOVE LEFT, TOP AND BOTTOM: Winner of four consecutive Gold Gloves (1973–76) and a three-time All-Star, Bobby Grich was part of the best infield in baseball through the first half of the 1970s. He set the major league fielding record (.995) for second basemen in 1973 and broke it twelve years later with the Angels (.997). He had a solid bat (.260 with the O's) and keen eye (.372 on-base percentage) and averaged 12 homers in his five full seasons with the club.

ABOVE: Left-hander Ross Grimsley was acquired from the Reds and went 18–13 in 1974, his first season with the Orioles. He went 50–43 in four seasons as a starter and returned to finish his career in the bullpen in 1982.

OPPOSITE TOP, LEFT AND RIGHT: Terry Crowley spent parts of 12 seasons with the Orioles and earned his nickname, "The King of Swing," as one of the top pinch-hitters in the game, recording 108 pinch hits over his career. He also was the first designated hitter in club history on April 6, 1973. The Crow later served as Orioles hitting coach from 1985–1988 and from 1999 to 2010.

OPPOSITE BOTTOM: After an MVP season at AAA Rochester in 1967, Curt Motton joined the Orioles and stayed five seasons as a reserve outfielder and pinch-hitter. His two-out pinch-hit single in the bottom of the eleventh inning gave the Orioles a 1–0 win in Game 2 of the 1969 ALCS against the Twins. He returned to the club for brief stints in 1973 and '74, and later scouted for the Orioles for more than twenty years.

TOP: Baltimore native Tim Nordbrook was called up to the Orioles in September 1974 and spent the next two seasons in the majors as a back-up infielder.
ABOVE: Had the designated hitter rule been in effect earlier, Don Baylor might have made the Orioles club sooner after two monster seasons at AAA Rochester in 1970 and 1971. Baylor played in six seasons with the Orioles before being traded to Oakland after the 1975 season.
OPPOSITE: Ross Grimsley went 50–43 in four seasons as a starter for the Orioles between 1974 and 1977, then he returned to finish his career as a reliever in 1982.

For the first time, Weaver's status as manager came into play. In mid-August, with his team on the verge of dropping completely out of the race, he addressed the issue: "The way I look at it," he said, "my job is always at stake if we don't win."

Almost on cue, and thanks in large part to a strong stretch run by Powell, in what would prove to be his swan song, the Orioles went on a pitching-induced tear that was highlighted by a Labor Day doubleheader sweep of the first-place Red Sox by identical 1–0 scores, with Mike Cuellar and Ross Grimsley authoring complete-game masterpieces. From a third-place standing, eight games back on August 28, the Orioles won 28 of their last 34 games to finish with a 91–71 record and a second straight divisional title, their fifth in the last six years.

By the end of the 1974 season, the Orioles had put 1972 in the rearview mirror, dismissing it as a fluke of offensive proportions, but they couldn't do the same with the rampaging A's, who won the ALCS in four games and went on to win their third straight World Series. Once again, the Orioles went to the off-season trade market. This time they made a couple of blockbusters plus a deal that finalized Boog Powell's colorful playing career in Baltimore, sending Powell to Cleveland in exchange for catcher Dave Duncan.

Powell's fate was sealed on December 3, 1974, when the Orioles sent Enos Cabell and infielder Rob Andrews to Houston for power-hitting first baseman Lee May. The Orioles topped that move the very next day, acquiring Ken Singleton and pitcher Mike Torrez from the Montreal Expos in exchange for Rich Coggins and Dave McNally. That deal turned out to be pivotal in the course of baseball history: McNally and the Dodgers' Andy Messersmith refused to sign contracts for the 1975 season, setting in motion the process that would bring free agency to baseball.

In the 1975 season, consistency would continue to be a trademark for the Orioles, despite a fourth straight slow start, which had become another trademark. At one point in mid-May, they lost 11 of 12, and even more troublesome, they blew eighth-inning leads in seven of their first 13 losses. Eventually the Orioles would get to 90 wins, as Palmer had a big bounce-back year with a 23–11 record and 2.09 ERA, and the key figures in the off-season trades played prominent roles.

May finished with 20 homers and 99 RBIs, Singleton hit .300, and Torrez was a sensational backup to Palmer with a 20–9, 3.06 ERA, season. In addition, Don Baylor showed his power potential for the first time by hitting 25 home runs. But the sluggish

start was too much to overcome, and the Orioles finished four-and-a-half games behind the Red Sox in a season that would go down as the lull before the storm.

In the middle of the 1975 season, team owner Jerry Hoffberger made the surprising announcement that the club was no longer for sale, perhaps because the family was in the process of selling the National Brewing Co., which had a connection to the club from the very beginning. Then, shortly after the World Series, Hoffberger made an even more startling revelation—that he was returning President Frank Cashen to his original position at the brewery. The move, which wouldn't have surprised anybody eight years earlier, was a shocker considering the uncertainty facing baseball at the time.

Into this void stepped Hank Peters as the Orioles' new vice president and general manager. Uncertainty abounded, particularly about the effect that impending free agency might have and about the possibility of an ownership change. Peters also faced a lot of homework while learning on the fly about the team he would be directing for the foreseeable future. A former minor league director for Charlie Finley's A's when they were in Kansas City, Peters came to the Orioles after serving as president of the National Association, the governing arm of baseball's minor league system. He came with a wealth of knowledge about running a franchise, but there were no guidelines for what he would face.

Free agency wouldn't be instituted until after the end of the 1976 season, so for the season itself, Peters concentrated on the needs of his club. For the first time in recent years, the Orioles made no significant trades during the winter months, but Peters wasted little time determining that obtaining a left-handed power hitter was a priority, and in no time he identified Reggie Jackson as a primary target.

A's owner Charlie Finley had already unloaded many of his marquee players, and Peters figured that Jackson would be next. Peters was the highest ranking member of Finley's front office when the A's drafted Jackson, so he knew dealing with either wouldn't be easy. He also knew he was in uncharted waters, but

TOP AND ABOVE: One of the major assets to the Orioles' winning ways in the late 1970s and early 1980s was Ken Singleton. Acquired from Montreal after the 1974 season for pitcher Dave McNally, "Singy" played outfield and later DH'd during his ten years with the club, batting .284 with 182 homers and 766 RBIs.
OPPOSITE TOP: Hank Peters was Orioles' vice president and general manager from November 1975 through November 1987, the longest tenure of anyone who has held the position for the club.
OPPOSITE BOTTOM: In helping the Orioles to the AL pennant in 1979, switch-hitting Ken Singleton finished second in AL MVP voting after batting .295 with career highs of 35 homers and 111 RBIs.

he stayed the course, and less than five months after taking the Orioles job, Peters pulled the trigger on a trade that not only jump-started his tenure in office but also set in motion a chain of events that would impact the Orioles for the next decade.

On April 2, 1976, just one week before the season opener, and within hours of the Orioles leaving spring training, the Orioles traded Don Baylor, Mike Torrez, and right-handed pitching prospect Paul Mitchell to the A's for Reggie Jackson and left-handed pitcher Ken Holtzman. It was a stunning trade, announced right after an exhibition game, and it generated an emotional scene rarely witnessed in a big-league clubhouse. Grown men didn't hide the tears as long-standing friendships—such as those experienced by Grich and Baylor, who had come up together in the O's organization, and Singleton and Torrez, teammates on two teams and one trade—were temporarily put on hold as careers changed directions.

Even Earl Weaver seemed affected by the reaction. As much as he looked forward to having Jackson in his lineup, he couldn't hide his admiration for Baylor's all-in style of play. "I told him he's going to be a Most Valuable Player some day," Weaver told a crowd of reporters after he had said his good-byes, "and I believe that, I really do." Four years later, Baylor proved him "really" right.

This trade was only a first step for Peters, but the next one was a long time coming. For the moment, Jackson took advantage of the timing of the trade, and the impending arrival of free agency, to hold out for what the Orioles thought was an unreasonable salary for the times—$200,000. The times . . . they were a-changing. It took more than a month to get Jackson to Baltimore, and by then Holtzman's dissatisfaction with not getting the same contractual consideration as Reggie assured there would be more wheeling and dealing by the June 15 trade deadline.

One trade that would have sent Holtzman to Kansas City fell through,

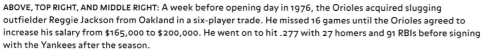

ABOVE, TOP RIGHT, AND MIDDLE RIGHT: A week before opening day in 1976, the Orioles acquired slugging outfielder Reggie Jackson from Oakland in a six-player trade. He missed 16 games until the Orioles agreed to increase his salary from $165,000 to $200,000. He went on to hit .277 with 27 homers and 91 RBIs before signing with the Yankees after the season.

BOTTOM RIGHT AND OPPOSITE: Left-hander Grant Jackson was a reliable reliever for the Orioles from 1971 into the 1976 season, going 24–12 with 39 saves and a 2.81 ERA in 209 games.

and then Peters pulled off a mammoth trade that not only justified his first one but provided the club with a foundational nucleus that would eventually produce two more pennants. Beating the deadline by only a couple of hours, the Orioles sent Ken Holtzman, Doyle Alexander, Grant Jackson, Elrod Hendricks, and minor league pitcher Jimmy Freeman to the Yankees in exchange for catcher Rick Dempsey, pitchers Rudy May, Tippy Martinez, and Dave Pagan, along with minor league pitcher Scott McGregor, who would turn out to be a key player in the trade.

The Orioles got a good year out of Reggie Jackson, who hit .277 with 27 home runs and 91 RBIs in 134 games, but it was the residual effect of that trade that best served the Orioles down the road. Lee May backed up his auspicious debut in Baltimore with 25 homers and 109 RBIs, while Jim Palmer continued his run with a 22–13, 2.51 ERA, record. The O's got an unexpected bonus when Wayne Garland finished 20–7, 2.67.

The unsettled start, at least in part influenced by Reggie's reluctance to join the party early, once again doomed the Orioles, who managed a second-place finish with an 88–74 record, 10½ games behind the runaway Yankees. And that wasn't even the bad news. What would happen next was anybody's guess, but it couldn't be any more chaotic than what had happened the previous five years.

Or could it?

MEMORABLE GAMES
1972-1976

June 16, 1973

Jim Palmer retires the first 25 Texas batters he faces before Rangers catcher Ken Suarez singles with one out in the ninth at Memorial Stadium. Palmer settles for a two-hit, 9–1 win.

October 10, 1973

A's pitcher Catfish Hunter shuts out the Orioles, 3–0, in the deciding Game 5 of the ALCS to deny the Orioles a trip to the World Series.

July 27, 1973

The Orioles beat the White Sox, 17–0, the largest shutout victory in club history. Pitcher Jim Hardin hits a three-run homer and tosses a two-hitter, retiring the last 20 Sox in order. Frank Robinson hits two homers and drives in five runs, and Mark Belanger has four hits.

October 9, 1974

After taking the first game of the ALCS, the Orioles drop three straight to the A's as Catfish Hunter again wins the clinching game, 2–1.

June 18, 1974

Bobby Grich becomes the first Oriole to hit three home runs in a game at Memorial Stadium to lead the O's to a 10–1 win over Minnesota.

August 9, 1975

Bobby Grich draws five consecutive walks in a 12–6 win at Chicago, the only time in club history a player has walked five times in a game. Jim Palmer gets the win, coming within one out of a complete game despite allowing six runs on 13 hits and three walks.

CHAPTER 8

THANKS, BROOKS! WELCOME EDDIE, EBW & O'S MAGIC

The uncertainty that pre-vailed during the 1976 season was a brush fire compared to the seven-alarmer that arrived in the ensuing off-season, when free agency transformed the structure of Major League Baseball. Players with at least six years of major league service were no longer bound by the reserve clause, which had bound players to their team since the beginning of baseball.

Instead, those veteran players were free to negotiate with other teams. Neither players nor owners knew what to expect or how to handle the wealth of talent suddenly available. There was a semblance of a draft that enabled teams to negotiate with selected players, but this did little to stem the immediate confusion of free agency.

In 1976, during his year in Baltimore, Reggie Jackson made the statement one day that if he played in New York, "they would name a candy bar after me." Then, as part of the first free agent class in 1977, Jackson did ink a deal with the New York Yankees, and a candy bar was named after him. For the most part, players on the move followed his lead and followed the money.

"Exactly what we figured would happen is what is happening," said General Manager Hank Peters as he tried to piece together his team. Not unexpectedly, the Orioles were among the teams hardest hit, losing Gold Glove second base-man Bobby Grich to the Angels and 20-game-winning pitcher Wayne Garland to the Indians in addition to Jackson. For the most part, however, Peters was able to keep the core of his team together, and the Orioles escaped the early days of free agency relatively unscathed, after the initial blow, even if it wasn't recognized as such at the time.

OPPOSITE: Eddie Murray gestures during the 1983 ALCS during Game 4 at Comiskey Park in Chicago.
FOLLOWING PAGES: The Orioles and the Pirates line up for Game 1 of the 1979 World Series at Memorial Stadium.

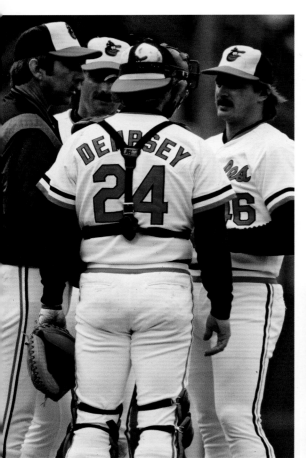

Outside of Baltimore, the Orioles were given little respect, and even on the home front there was some feeling of despair. As the 1977 season approached, the Orioles were virtually dismissed as contenders for the first time since 1968. Paul Blair had been traded to the Yankees, Mike Cuellar had been waived, and 39-year-old Brooks Robinson, having been replaced as starting third baseman by Doug DeCinces, was in a new position as a player-coach, mostly in a reserve role.

Jackson was one of the first to write the Orioles off as challengers in the American League East. "I don't think they can compete with what they have," he said, when asked to appraise his former team. "I would think fourth place, maybe third, is the best they can do."

The comment didn't go over well with Reggie's ex-teammates, the most outspoken of whom was Lee May, not normally one to make waves or acknowledge them. "Who cares what Reggie thinks," said the veteran first baseman. "He's not here. What does he know?"

TOP: (Left to right) Ray Miller with Doug DeCinces, Rick Dempsey, and Mike Flanagan in 1979, served three stints as Orioles pitching coach spanning 11 seasons.

ABOVE: Don Stanhouse, the Orioles closer in 1978–79, got the nickname "Fullpack" for his propensity to put runners on base before saving the game, causing manager Earl Weaver to go through a full pack of cigarettes in the dugout in the ninth inning. He racked up 45 saves and a 2.87 ERA in his two seasons as closer.

RIGHT: After nine years as a utility player with the Indians and Rangers, John Lowenstein joined the Orioles for the 1979 season and platooned in left field for seven seasons. "Brother Lo" batted .274 with 68 homers in that time, and his three-run pinch-hit homer in Game 1 of the 1979 ALCS led to a sweep of the Angels.

ABOVE: Known as the "Throwin' Swannanoan" after his hometown of Swannanoa, North Carolina, Sammy Stewart set a major league record by striking out six consecutive White Sox batters in his first game on September 1, 1978. He pitched in a variety of roles, mostly in long relief, over the next seven seasons and appeared to have won the league ERA title in 1981 with a 2.32 ERA. However, under the rules at the time, innings pitched were rounded to the nearest full inning; Stewart "lost" one-third of an inning and Oakland's Steve McCatty gained one-third, leaving the A's hurler at 2.32 and Stewart at 2.33. The rule was changed after that season.

As it turned out, Jackson, and many others, would later admit to underrating the Orioles. A big reason why they did was a twenty-year-old named Eddie Murray. After a year and a half in AA and a half season in AAA in the minors, Murray arrived at the big-league spring training camp in 1977. Two years earlier, at the urging of then-minor league coach Cal Ripken Sr., Murray had taken up switch-hitting, and it was a smart move: the Orioles still needed a left-handed hitter, which they had been seeking when they traded for Reggie Jackson the year before.

Murray was ticketed for a return to Triple-A in 1977, but the more Weaver saw of him in spring training, the more he liked, and the harder he campaigned to take the rookie to Baltimore. "The people who overlooked us weren't paying attention," said Weaver. "We lost three good players, but we still had a lot of good people, and some others on the way up."

The most significant of those "on the way up" was Murray, and Weaver used an unusual ploy in an effort to ease the rookie's transition—using him as the designated hitter and leaving Lee May at first base, a tactic he used throughout the 1977 season. It worked to perfection, as May again drove in 99 runs, with 27 home runs. Murray matched May's home run total and drove in 88 runs, which earned him Rookie of the Year honors. Murray was a key element during the Orioles' surprising run at the Yankees, who didn't clinch until the next to last day of the season. Meanwhile, the Orioles and Red Sox tied for second with identical 97–64 records. The race was succinctly summarized by Boston manager Don Zimmer.

"No team that wins 97 games should finish in third place," Zimmer said after the teams had played game number 161. "We've had too good a season to finish third, and so has Baltimore." Which is why nobody seemed disappointed when the final game of the season between the Orioles and Red Sox was rained out.

In what amounted to a makeover year for the Orioles, with one future Hall of Famer (Murray) arriving as another was leaving, two final, defining

OPPOSITE TOP: In addition to giving Brooks Robinson the nickname "Hoover" after being robbed of hits repeatedly with the Reds in the 1970 World Series, Lee May spent six years with the Orioles (1976–80) and helped tutor Eddie Murray when the future Hall of Famer made the leap to the majors in 1977. May averaged 20 homers and 81 RBIs with the Orioles and was voted Most Valuable Oriole in 1976 when he hit 25 homers and led the AL with 109 RBIs.

OPPOSITE BOTTOM: Mike Flanagan won 141 games in fifteen seasons with the Orioles, thirteen as a starter from 1975 to 1987 and two as a left-handed reliever in 1991–92. He won the 1979 Cy Young Award when he went 23–9 with a 3.08 ERA and led the AL with five shutouts.

LEFT AND ABOVE: The last player to wear No. 8 for the Orioles before Cal Ripken Jr., Dave Skaggs spent seven seasons in the minors before reaching the majors as back-up catcher in 1977. He caught 80 games and hit .287 as a rookie, but would play only 101 more games with the Orioles before being sold to the Angels in May 1980.

moments of Brooks Robinson's legendary career served as bookends for this rather remarkable season. Pinch-hitting against the Indians in the 10th inning on April 19, 1977, Brooks delivered a game-winning, three-run homer, the 268th and last of his career, a dramatic event Weaver called his "biggest thrill in baseball." Five months later, on September 18, 51,798 fans filled Memorial Stadium for "Thanks, Brooks Day," a fitting end to his twenty-three-year career, which had all been spent in the same uniform.

During the 1978 season, the loss of Al Bumbry to a broken ankle proved to be a major bump in the road, as the fleet outfielder was restricted to only 33 games. The first week of the season also featured a failed experiment of Murray playing third base, a move abandoned after an opening three-game sweep in Milwaukee.

For the season, Doug DeCinces stepped up as Brooks's heir at third base and hit 28 home runs, 80 RBIs, and had a .286 batting average, which supplemented the home run power of Murray (27), May (25), and Singleton (20). However, the Orioles suffered a significant drop in run production (719 to 659) and dropped to fourth place, despite a more than respectable 90–71 record.

The exodus of several free agents paid an indirect dividend in the form of compensation picks in the June 1978 amateur draft. The Orioles received three

additional picks in the second round, and with their third pick of the round they took Cal Ripken Jr., a selection of historic importance.

As the 1979 season unfolded, talk was renewed that owner Jerry Hoffberger was intent on selling the team. Even as the Orioles reestablished themselves as legitimate contenders, questions about the team's ownership and even its future in Baltimore dominated the headlines.

Then, on August 2, 1979, the sale of the team to famed Washington-based attorney Edward Bennett Williams was announced. Speculation ran rampant that the team would play some of its home games in the District of Columbia and eventually move there, leading *The News American* to headline its story of the sale "Bye-Bye Birdies." The prospect of playing some games in Washington met resistance from the Major League Baseball Players Association, but it didn't diminish the possibility of a move to DC—despite Williams's statement that he "didn't buy the team to move it," to which he added, "as long as the people of Baltimore support the Orioles, they will stay here." Further fanning speculation was the fact that commissioner Bowie Kuhn was on record as favoring a Baltimore-Washington area team.

The local populace made a statement in the only way that mattered—at the gate. From a very modest total of 1,051,724 in 1978, regular-season attendance jumped to 1,681,009 in 1979, a mark that has been surpassed every season with at least 75 home dates since then.

In the meantime, despite another of their patented slow starts, which saw them lose eight of their first 11 games, the Orioles were riding Weaver's favorite pattern of "pitching, defense, and three-run homers." It was the year that "Orioles Magic" came into being, fueled by a series of dramatic wins and the "Roar from 34," a regular and growing crowd of fans seated in upper section 34 at Memorial Stadium who were led in cheers by super-fan Wild Bill Hagy, a local cab driver.

An early nine-game winning streak came in the midst of a stretch that produced 19 wins in 22 games and carried the Orioles into first place on June 5, 1979, and they never looked back. They posted a 23–6 record for the month of June, when DeCinces and Murray both produced game-winning homers in the ninth inning on consecutive nights to beat the Tigers and give birth to "Orioles Magic."

For the season, pitcher Mike Flanagan finished 23–9 and won the Cy Young Award as the Orioles' offense enjoyed a resurgence, scoring 759 runs as Ken Singleton (.295, 35 HRs, 111 RBIs) had a career year, and Murray had another consistent year (.295, 25 HRs, and 99 RBIs). However, it was in left field that the team's "deep depth" provided the most eye-popping numbers, as Gary Roenicke and John Lowenstein combined for 36 home runs and 98 runs batted in.

OPPOSITE: With Cal Ripken Jr. ready to take over third base in 1982, the Orioles traded Doug DeCinces to the Angels for veteran outfielder Dan Ford. Ford would be a key player during the 1983 championship season, batting .280 with 55 RBIs, but was injured for much of his four seasons with the Orioles.

ABOVE: Third base coach Cal Ripken Sr. gives an "atta boy" to son Cal Jr. after the rookie's opening day home run against the Royals in 1982. Cal Sr., who began his career as a minor league catcher, spent thirty-six years in the Orioles organization, including fifteen years on the major league coaching staff and one year and six games as manager.

An early nine-game winning streak came in the midst of a stretch that produced 19 wins in 22 games and carried the Orioles into first place on June 5, 1979, and they never looked back. They posted a 23-6 record for the month of June, when DeCinces and Murray both produced game-winning homers in the ninth inning on consecutive nights to beat the Tigers and give birth to 'Orioles Magic.'"

ABOVE: Not only did Doug DeCinces replace a legend when he took over third base from Brooks Robinson in the mid-1970s but he was traded after the 1981 season to make room for another legend at the hot corner, rookie Cal Ripken Jr. DeCinces played nine seasons with the Orioles, and his two-out, two-run homer to beat the Tigers on June 22, 1979, gave rise to "Orioles Magic."

The end result was a 102–57 record in 1979 that enabled the Orioles to breeze to another Eastern Division title. They went on to win a fifth American League pennant, beating the California Angels in four games. That set up another exciting but ultimately disappointing World Series matchup against the Pittsburgh Pirates. After splitting the first two games, the Orioles hammered out 8–4 and 9–6 wins to build a 3-to-1 advantage, but that was as close as they got. They scored only two runs over the final three games as the Pirates won them all, including another Game 7 classic, as Willie Stargell's two-run homer topped a four-hit night in a 4–1 victory that delivered Pittsburgh the series.

As an encore to their pennant-winning year in 1979, the Orioles compiled a 100–62 record in 1980 that featured many breakthrough individual seasons. However, the Yankees went 103–59 that year, and the Orioles were eliminated on the next to last day of the season for the second time in four years. Having grown tired of hearing about "slow starts," Manager Earl Weaver repeatedly responded to questions demanding an explanation by asking: "What is a slow start? How many games count as a start?" There were no answers or explanations, only the hard fact that the Orioles won 52 of their last 72 games, but it wasn't enough.

In the 1980 season, pitcher Steve Stone, a free-agent acquisition two years earlier, posted a 25–7 record and a 3.23 ERA, which earned him the Cy Young Award, and pitcher Scott McGregor finished with a personal best 20–8 record and a 3.32 ERA. This was the last season in a remarkable streak of thirteen consecutive years that the Orioles had at least one 20-game winner. Offensively, Al Bumbry showed how much he meant to the team's offense, becoming the first player in club history to surpass 200 hits (with 205) en route to a .318 average while scoring 118 of the team's 805 runs.

OPPOSITE: Scott McGregor pitches in Game 5 of the 1983 World Series at Philadelphia, during which he shut out the Phillies, 5–0, in the final game. McGregor had a 1.63 ERA in six postseason starts, pitching 49 2/3 of a possible 54 innings.
BELOW: Manager Joe Altobelli (left) and General Manager Hank Peters celebrate beating the White Sox to win the 1983 ALCS and advance to the World Series.

ABOVE: Kiko Garcia, a part-time infielder from 1976 to 1980, likely would have been the 1979 World Series MVP had the Orioles beaten the Pirates, as he batted .400 and drove in a team-leading 6 RBIs.

OPPOSITE: Rookie Cal Ripken Jr. warms up between innings in 1981. Brought up as a third baseman, Ripken moved to shortstop in 1982 and changed the image of the prototypical shortstop. At 6′4″, Ripken had superior range and athleticism for someone that size playing the position. He would be the model of consistency throughout his twenty-one-year career, winning two MVP awards (in 1983 and 1991) and two Gold Gloves.

Eddie Murray (.300, 32 HRs, 116 RBIs, 100 runs scored) continued his remarkable run; Ken Singleton hit .304 with 24 homers and 104 RBIs; and Terry Crowley took advantage of 233 at-bats as the part-time designated hitter to log career highs with 12 home runs and 50 RBIs. In the end, though, it was another "close but no cigar" season.

Over the previous four years leading up to the 1981 season, the Orioles had 389 wins but only one pennant to show for it. This was adequate testimony to both excellence and frustration, which were rapidly becoming team trademarks. Then the 1981 season was marred by a different frustration: another players' strike that split the season in half—and left the Orioles with an empty feeling once again.

When the work stoppage began on June 12, 1981, the Orioles were 31–23, two games behind the Yankees. Games resumed on July 31, and the Orioles went 28–23 in the "second half." They finished two games behind the Milwaukee Brewers, who would eventually lose to the Yankees in a playoff between the two division "winners." Because of a bizarre schedule imbalance, the Orioles played two games fewer than the first place teams in a strike-shortened season that saw teams play between 103 and 109 games.

Owner Edward Williams was instrumental in helping resolve the long-running labor dispute, though it didn't salvage his team's season. Nevertheless, there were a few highlights. Cal Ripken Jr. made his big-league debut that season, scoring the winning run as a 12th-inning pinch-runner (for Singleton) on August 10, 1981. The irony of the shortened season is that Murray, who had signed a five-year contract, was in the midst of what undoubtedly would have been his breakthrough year, as he led the American League with 22 home runs and 78 RBIs. Pitcher Dennis Martinez led the league in wins with his 14–5 record, but the individual honors went for naught, and the Orioles were once again left to ponder what might have been.

Then, before the start of the 1982 season, Weaver expressed his intention to retire. He said 1982 would be his last as the Orioles manager, and Williams tried unsuccessfully to talk his manager out of his decision. Despite his owner's pleas, Weaver held firm with his plans, which may or may not have been a factor in what was a rather lethargic 1982 season until the final month.

With DeCinces having been traded, Ripken opened the season at third base, but he was eventually moved to shortstop as Weaver sought ways to increase offensive output. By season's end, Ripken was named the American League Rookie of the Year, hitting .264 with 28 home runs and 93 runs batted in. Murray had his breakout year (.316, 32 HRs, 110 RBIs), while Lowenstein (24 HRs, 66 RBIs) and Roenicke (21 HRs, 74 RBIs) provided 45 home runs and 140 runs batted in a dynamic platoon in left field.

After a furious late-season stretch run, in which they went 33–10, the Orioles were in contention to win the Eastern Division on the season's final weekend, a showdown with the first-place Brewers. The Orioles were three games back with four games to play and needed a sweep. When the O's swept a doubleheader on Friday and followed that with an 11–3 win on Saturday, it set up a winner-take-all contest for the season's last game.

However, the Brewers jumped out to a quick lead and cruised to a 10–2 win, leaving the hometown O's crowd of 51,462 with nothing to cheer for except the manager's career. And they did just that, staying put for a prolonged period of time until Weaver, his face smeared with tears, returned to the field to acknowledge a crowd that wasn't ready for him to leave.

OPPOSITE: Cal Ripken Jr. was the 1982 AL Rookie of the Year and went on to win two MVP awards during his 21-year career. But, of course, he is best known for breaking "The Streak" previously held by Lou Gehrig, eventually playing 2,632 consecutive games.
ABOVE LEFT: An eight-year veteran with a lackluster 67–72 record when he joined the Orioles in 1979, Steve Stone had a season for the ages in 1980, his second of three seasons with the Birds. Using a sneaky fastball and devastating curve, he went 25–7 with a 3.23 ERA, pitched a career-high 250 1/3 innings, won the Cy Young Award, and started the All-Star Game for the AL. The curveballs took a toll, however, as he developed arm trouble the next spring and went just 4–7, ending his career. His 25 wins in '80 are the most in Orioles history, and his winning percentage of .656 (40–21) is the highest by an Oriole with 40 or more decisions with the club.
ABOVE: Perhaps no one epitomized the town he played in more than Rick Dempsey, who caught more games than anyone in his 12 seasons in an Orioles uniform. The MVP of the 1983 World Series, Dempsey caught six different 20-game winners with the Orioles.

ABOVE: Gary Roenicke formed the right-handed half of the left-field platoon, hitting 118 homers from 1978 to 1985. In 1982, he hit .270 with 21 homers and 74 RBIs, and he followed that in 1983 with .260, 19 HR, 64 RBI season.

RIGHT: One of the top relievers in club history, left-hander Tippy Martinez saved 105 games in 11 seasons with the Orioles (1976–86). In the 10th inning of a game against Toronto on August 24, 1983, he got three outs without retiring a batter, picking off three Toronto runners at first base. In Game 4 of the 1983 ALCS at Chicago, he pitched four shutout innings to clinch the pennant for the Orioles.

But leave Weaver did, if only temporarily as it turned out. For the 1983 season, not much changed when Joe Altobelli moved into the manager's office. The coaching staff stayed intact. Altobelli was a product of "The Oriole Way," having managed in the system before with the Triple-A farm team in Rochester, which had also been Weaver's last stop before coming to Baltimore.

It wasn't the worst-case scenario for Altobelli, who inherited a team that had the second-best record in baseball in 1982, and despite some injuries to the pitching staff, the Orioles had enough firepower to continue as a contender, even as the team seemed to be running a tryout camp in an effort to find a regular third baseman. It was a versatile team, with veteran leadership, emerging superstars in Murray and Ripken, and like its immediate predecessors, an ability to finish strong, which it needed.

The Orioles were in fourth place, one game out of first in the tight AL East and riding a seven-game losing streak heading into their game at Chicago on August 13, 1983. With Jim Palmer unable to start due to an injury, rookie Bill Swaggerty made his big league debut and held the White Sox at bay for six innings. The Orioles eventually won the game, 5–2, and from there went 34–10 over the next six weeks to clinch the division title with a week left in the season.

LEFT: Tito Landrum became a Baltimore hero when his 10th inning home run in Game 4 of the 1983 ALCS broke a scoreless tie and launched the Orioles into the World Series.
ABOVE: Rick Dempsey spent nearly half of his twenty-four-year career with the Orioles. Though he hit only .238 in 12 seasons with the Birds, he batted .385 with 4 doubles and a homer to earn World Series MVP honors in 1983.

> "With Sox starter Britt Burns still on the mound, unheralded outfielder Tito Landrum, acquired only hours before the August 31 trade deadline, unloaded with a home run into the upper deck at Comiskey Park, giving the Orioles the lead."

After losing the first game of the ALCS against the White Sox, Mike Boddicker struck out 14 batters in a complete game shutout to even the series, and Murray hit a three-run homer in the first inning of Game 3 to start an 11–1 rout. Game 4 was pivotal, as the Orioles did not want to face the eventual Cy Young Award winner, Chicago's Lamarr Hoyt, if the series went to five games.

Game 4 was as dramatic as any the Orioles have ever played, going scoreless into the 10th inning. With Sox starter Britt Burns still on the mound, unheralded outfielder Tito Landrum, acquired only hours before the August 31 trade deadline, unloaded with a home run into the upper deck at Comiskey Park, giving the Orioles the lead. They added two more runs to win, 3–0, and advance to the World Series for a sixth time.

As with the league series, the Orioles dropped the opener to the National League champion Philadelphia Phillies before Boddicker evened things up in the next game with a complete game victory. From there, the Orioles won a pair of one-run games to take a 3–1 lead. In Game 5, Murray blasted two homers and eventual World Series MVP Rick Dempsey added another as the Orioles won, 5–0, and closed out the World Series in five games.

OPPOSITE TOP: Rick Dempsey (right) gives Scott McGregor a bear hug after the Orioles shut out the Phillies in Game 5 of the 1983 World Series.

OPPOSITE BOTTOM: Commissioner Bowie Kuhn (far left) presents the 1983 World Series trophy to (left to right) Orioles' Manager Joe Altobelli, General Manager Hank Peters, owner Edward Bennett Williams, and World Series MVP Rick Dempsey.

ABOVE: Orioles' Manager Joe Altobelli is congratulated by White Sox Manager Tony LaRussa after the Birds beat Chicago in the 1983 ALCS.

BELOW: The Orioles celebrate their third World Series title in 1983.

In 1983, Ripken put together an MVP year (.318, 27 HRs, 102 RBIs), and he led the league in runs scored (121), hits (211), doubles (47), and games played, the latter a trend that would define his career. Murray, still the most consistent hitter in the game, hit 33 home runs, drove in 111, scored 115, and hit .306. Meanwhile, Lowenstein (15 HRs, 60 RBIs) and Roenicke (19 HRs, 64 RBIs) remained the game's best left-field combination, totaling 34 HRs and 124 RBIs.

On the mound, Scott McGregor fashioned an 18–7 record with a 3.18 ERA; Mike Flanagan bounced back from injuries for a 12–4, 3.30 ERA, line; Storm Davis went 13–7, 3.59; and Boddicker, who started the season in the minors, made a big impact with a 16–8, 2.77 mark. Tippy Martinez emerged as a reliable closer in the bullpen, posting 21 saves to go with a 9–3 record and 2.35 ERA.

For Altobelli and the Orioles, 1983 was a magical year. It began with Brooks Robinson's election to the Hall of Fame and culminated with a World Series triumph over the Phillies.

In retrospect, the run by the Best Damn Team in Baseball proved to be much more than a three-year winning streak. In actuality it covered two decades—starting with the coming out party in 1964 and running through that magical 1983 season.

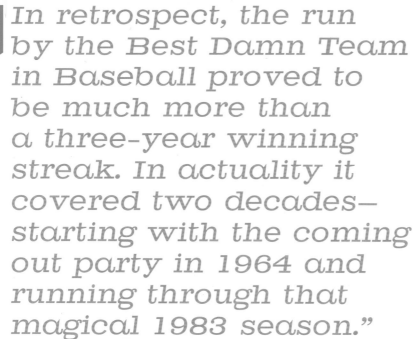

" In retrospect, the run by the Best Damn Team in Baseball proved to be much more than a three-year winning streak. In actuality it covered two decades—starting with the coming out party in 1964 and running through that magical 1983 season."

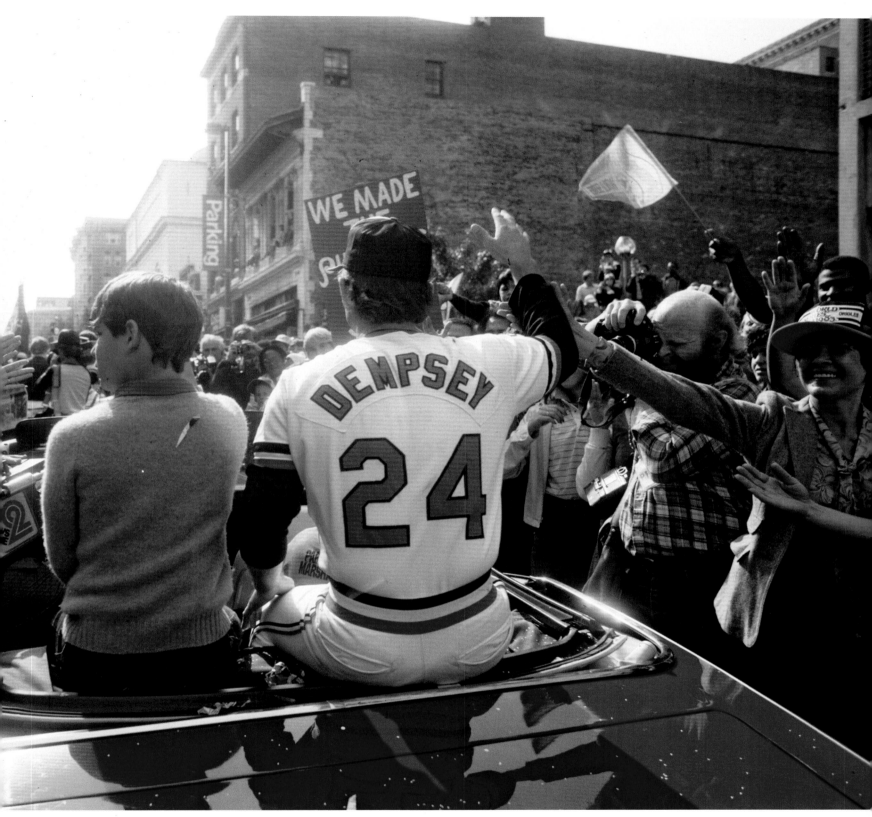

OPPOSITE LEFT: The newspaper headline says it all—fans and ushers celebrate the Orioles' 1983 World Series victory.

ABOVE: Rick Dempsey and his son, John, wave to fans during the 1983 World Series parade through downtown Baltimore.

LEFT: And a cab driver shall lead them . . . "Wild Bill" Hagy and some of the "Roar from 34" had their own ride in the 1983 World Series parade. Hagy led cheers in Section 34 at Memorial Stadium for many years, contorting his body to form the letters O-R-I-O-L-E-S.

DOUG DECINCES:
THE START OF ORIOLES MAGIC

PROFILE

For the educated Baltimore baseball fan, June 22, 1979, is etched in club history as the day "Orioles Magic" was born.

For Doug DeCinces, that date will always seem like yesterday. "I still get chills just thinking about it," said the former O's third baseman and member of the club's Hall of Fame whose dramatic ninth-inning, two-out, two-run home run was the blast that provided the impetus for a wild and wacky weekend that stands as a turning point in the franchise's proud history.

That weekend took place in the midst of what was an unsettling time for the Orioles, who were in the process of an ownership change from Jerry Hoffberger to Edward Bennett Williams.

"It was an unusual time for the club," DeCinces recalled. "There had been some talk of playing games in Washington. Those games [the weekend of June 22–24] seemed to get the city excited, the crowds got us excited, and it was just a very exciting time for everybody. It was a great experience being part of it."

The fact that DeCinces was even involved in the magical weekend was something of an upset, as he had played only sparingly to that point. "I hurt my back on a West Coast trip and was out for more than a month and had been struggling when I first came back," recalled DeCinces, who went 0-for-14 after returning to the lineup and saw his average dip to .190 by June 8.

It was as if the parade started without him and he was trying to catch up. He got his chance in that game on June 22, after Ken Singleton had hit a one-out home run to cut the Tigers' lead to 5–4, and Eddie Murray followed with a single. DeCinces came to the plate with two outs.

"I had been really anxious, probably overanxious, to do something—and when I got into the batter's box all I was thinking was, 'Here's my chance to do something to help the team,'" said DeCinces. He couldn't have written a better script.

DeCinces got a pitch to his liking from right-hander Dave Tobik and swung himself into a place in Orioles' lore. "I knew it was gone as soon as I hit it," he said, "and after that everything seemed like a blur. The crowd went crazy and the next thing I remembered was the whole team being at home plate. That didn't happen very often—we didn't have 'walkoffs' back then."

After doing a brief radio interview on the field, DeCinces retreated to a tumultuous clubhouse, only to be quickly summoned back onto the field. "Somebody came and got me and said, 'You've got to come out, they won't leave,' and I couldn't believe what I saw when I went back. The crowd was still going crazy. I went back to the clubhouse and said, 'Guys, you've got to come out and see this.' It was an unbelievable experience."

The crowd no doubt thought this was a once-in-a-lifetime, or certainly a once-in-a-season, experience, but for the Orioles and their suddenly frenzied fans, the fun had just begun. The very next night, in the first game of a doubleheader, with two men on base, two outs in the bottom of the ninth inning, and the Orioles trailing 6–5, Eddie Murray connected for a three-run homer off Tigers' relief ace John Hiller, and pandemonium broke loose once again.

No doubt buoyed by events of the night before, a crowd in excess of 45,000 witnessed Murray's heroics. Probably the only reason order was restored in a timely fashion was the fact that there was another game to be played. That one couldn't top the theatrics of the previous two games, but it still provided its own drama as Terry Crowley's pinch-hit single in the bottom of the eighth inning produced yet another win for the Orioles. It completed a trifecta of excitement never matched in club history—and signaled the birth of "Orioles Magic."

"It was a special time," said DeCinces. "That's when Wild Bill Hagy and the 'Roar from 34' became famous, and it just seemed to take off. We were pretty much a new team and had the feeling 'this is our time.' We just had such great camaraderie; we believed we could win those games. And we could sense that the crowds felt that way, too.

"One thing about that [June 22] game—we had been behind the whole game, but nobody left. It was a bigger crowd than usual, and they just hung in there. It was almost as if they were expecting something special to happen. It was an even bigger crowd the next night, and when Eddie hit his homer, it was magical. To have been part of all that is awesome."

DeCinces ranks the home run that helped set off "Orioles Magic" behind only the one he hit in his first at-bat in the 1979 World Series. "A few years ago, my daughter put together a series of clips from my career, and I get to listen once in a while with my grandchildren," said DeCinces. "I still get a thrill when I hear it—I'm not embarrassed to say I get emotional listening to it. And to think that all these years later people still talk about it—it's an unbelievable feeling."

Although he is third on the Orioles' all-time list with 105 career saves, Tippy Martinez would earn a place in the record books in 1983 by picking three runners off first base in the same inning. Perhaps he also deserves an asterisk as the winning pitcher in the two games that jump-started Orioles Magic.

OPPOSITE AND ABOVE: Doug DeCinces

MEMORABLE GAMES
1977–1983

June 22, 1979

Third baseman Doug DeCinces hits a dramatic two-out, two-run home run in the bottom of the ninth in front of more than 35,000 fans at Memorial Stadium, giving birth to "Orioles Magic." The Orioles trail 5–3 entering the ninth, but Ken Singleton homers and Eddie Murray singles before DeCinces's game-winning blast.

September 18, 1977

A crowd of 51,798 fans show up at Memorial Stadium on "Thanks, Brooks Day," honoring the Orioles third baseman who was placed on the voluntarily retired list four weeks earlier. During pregame ceremonies, Doug DeCinces, who had replaced Robinson as the starter that season, speaks for his teammates by simply pulling up third base and giving it to the future Hall of Famer.

August 13, 1978

The Yankees score five runs in the top of the seventh inning to take a 5–3 lead, but a heavy rain soaks Memorial Stadium and the game is called following a thirty-six-minute rain delay. Following MLB rules at the time, the score reverts to the previous inning and the Orioles win, 3–0, giving Scott McGregor his first lifetime victory over the team that signed him. The rule is later changed, and such games are now "suspended" and resumed from the point of the delay.

October 3, 1979

John Lowenstein's dramatic three-run pinch-hit homer in the 10th inning gives the Orioles a walk-off 6–3 win in the first game of the 1979 ALCS, and the Orioles go on to beat the Angels in four games and win the American League pennant.

October 17, 1979

The Orioles take a 3-games-to-1 lead over Pittsburgh in the World Series, only to have the Pirates come back to win the final three games. Eddie Murray's bases-loaded drive in the eighth inning of the last game is hauled in by Dave Parker, and the Pirates win the finale, 4–1.

October 8, 1983

In Game 4 of the ALCS, the O's Tito Landrum leads off the 10th inning at Comiskey Park with a home run into a stiff wind off Chicago's Britt Burns, breaking a scoreless tie, and the Orioles go on to a 3–0 victory to win the series, 3-games-to-1.

August 13, 1983

Called up to fill in for the injured Jim Palmer, Bill Swaggerty allows one run over six innings in his big-league debut at Chicago, and the Orioles beat the White Sox, 5–2, breaking a seven-game losing streak. They win 34 of their next 44 games to clinch the American League East with a week to go in the season.

October 16, 1983

Scott McGregor tosses a five-hit shutout, Eddie Murray homers twice, and World Series MVP Rick Dempsey also homers as the Orioles beat the Phillies in Game 5, 5–0, at Veterans Stadium, for their third World Series title.

July 1, 1982

Orioles manager Earl Weaver stuns the baseball establishment, moving third baseman Cal Ripken Jr. to shortstop to start a game against Cleveland. Ripken, whose legendary consecutive-games streak began 28 games earlier on May 30, would start the next 2,216 games at shortstop before moving back to third base to start a game.

August 24, 1983

After the Orioles tie the game against Toronto in the ninth inning and run out of position players, outfielders John Lowenstein and Gary Roenicke are forced to play the infield, and utility infielder Lenn Sakata enters as catcher. In the top of the 10th inning, Toronto retakes the lead before reliever Tippy Martinez enters and picks off three runners at first base to end the inning. Martinez first picks off Barry Bonnell at first. Then Jesse Barfield walks and is replaced by pinch-runner Dave Collins, who gets picked off. Finally, Willie Upshaw singles and is then picked off. In the bottom of the 10th, Cal Ripken homers to tie the game, and Sakata hits a game-winning three-run homer for a 7–4 win.

CHAPTER 9

MEMORIAL DAYS

The ink from the headline celebrating the Orioles' 1983 World Series championship hadn't dried yet when Rick Dempsey said the words that were more prophetic than he could have ever imagined. The improbable but wildly popular MVP of the O's triumph was slumped in the chair in front of his locker when he made a very simple declaration.

Less than two hours after the highlight of his career, the colorful catcher was already looking ahead. "Now," he proclaimed as the last drops of champagne dripped from his head, "comes the hard part—doing it again." Little did Dempsey know just how difficult that task would be—or that a period of decay would eventually set in and lead to a record-setting losing streak before the O's could get back on track.

In 1984, the Detroit Tigers broke from the gate with a 35–5 record, and other signs came early and often that repeating as champions was not going to be a viable option for the Orioles. The success of 1983 was the end of an era. Six weeks into the season, Jim Palmer, who only seven months earlier had become the first pitcher ever to win a World Series game in three successive decades, announced his retirement, and some of the other veterans showed signs of decline.

Not so, however, with Eddie Murray, who put together a season that might've landed him the Most Valuable Player Award that always seemed to just elude him, despite the fact that he garnered more MVP votes than any player over a ten-year period (finishing seven times in the top eight between 1978 and 1985). His 1984 season included a .306 batting average, 29 home runs, and 110 runs batted in, along with .410 on-base and .509 slugging percentages. His league-leading 25 intentional walks was another indication of his impact in the middle of a declining lineup that scored 118 fewer runs (for a total of 681) than the 1983 team.

OPPOSITE: Rick Dempsey (left) and Rich Dauer admire their 1983 World Series rings during opening day ceremonies in 1984.

Mike Boddicker had a breakout year, leading the pitching staff with a 20–11 record and 2.79 ERA, but manager Joe Altobelli never found a reliable fifth starter, and the drop off in run production took its toll. The 85–77 record in 1984 itself wasn't a disaster, but it resulted in only a fifth-place finish, as the Tigers kept the rest of the American League East at bay.

With attendance surpassing two million for the second straight year, owner Edward Bennett Williams vowed that he had no intention of moving the team, and he rejuvenated talks about a new stadium and proposed sites. He also turned attention to the club's immediate future. The Orioles hoped to use a trip to Japan, a result of their 1983 World Series victory, as a tryout of sorts for products of the minor league system, but that produced only mild results.

Only Larry Sheets emerged as a bright prospect for the upcoming 1985 season, and so Williams authorized General Manager Hank Peters to take a plunge into the free-agent pool. After the team acquired outfielders Fred Lynn and Lee Lacy and relief pitcher Don Aase, expectations quickly rose to 1983 heights, putting even more of a burden on Altobelli to produce a winner.

Williams had always been impressed with Earl Weaver's abilities. The former manager had retired early, at the age of fifty-two, and so the possibility of a return loomed practically from the time of his departure. This added to the pressure on Altobelli, which was magnified when Frank Robinson was added to the 1985 staff to serve as bench coach—apparently at the sole request of the owner.

On the surface at least, Altobelli was at ease with the move. "If I don't win, they'll find somebody else. It's as simple as that," he said. "Frank would be a candidate no matter where he was working." But with a revamped offense and a veteran starting rotation, the Orioles were a consensus pick to win the AL East. If they didn't win, there was little doubt the affable manager's job would be on the line.

TOP LEFT: Mike Boddicker was recalled in May 1983 and went on to win 16 games, including a league-leading five shutouts, and earn ALCS MVP honors with a 14-strikeout shutout against the White Sox.
TOP RIGHT: The Orioles signed nine-time All-Star Fred Lynn to a four-year free agent contract before the 1985 season to provide a middle-of-the-order bat and strong center-field defense. When healthy, he did that—hitting 23 homers in each of his three full seasons and 18 before being traded in August 1988 to Detroit—but he missed more than a season's worth of games in his time with the Orioles.
ABOVE: A former big league pitcher who once threw a no-hitter for the Brooklyn Dodgers, Rex Barney was the Orioles much-beloved public address announcer for nearly twenty-five years before his sudden passing on August 11, 1997. His signature calls of "Give that fan a contract" and a drawn out "Thank youuu" were well known beyond Memorial Stadium and Camden Yards.

PREVIOUS TOP: The Orioles' three World Series MVPs (left to right)—Brooks Robinson ('70), Rick Dempsey ('83), and Frank Robinson ('66)—gather in 1984.

PREVIOUS BOTTOM: Local product Jim Traber, from Columbia, Maryland, had several highlights in his four seasons with the Orioles (1984, '86, '88, '89), including singing the national anthem at Memorial Stadium before his big league debut on September 21, 1984. In 1986 he led AL rookies in homers per at bat (16.2) and was second among all AL players in RBIs per at bat (14.8).

TOP: Dave Schmidt went 28–23 with a 4.39 ERA in three seasons with the Orioles, twice finishing with double-digit win totals. He was the starter and winner when the 1988 Orioles broke their major league record, season-opening 21-game losing streak.

ABOVE: Storm Davis was nicknamed "Cy Clone" for his resemblance to Jim Palmer while starting for the Orioles from 1982 through 1986.

ABOVE RIGHT: Don Aase spent four years with the Orioles, from 1985 to 1988, making the All-Star team and earning 34 saves in 1986.

The first warning that the season wouldn't go smoothly came when left-hander Mike Flanagan popped an Achilles tendon in a team sanctioned off-season basketball game, which limited him to only 15 starts for the year. The void in the rotation was never adequately filled, and the team ERA jumped to 4.38 (from 3.71 the previous year), off-setting a jump in offensive production (to 818 runs).

On June 13, 1985, following a five-game losing streak that dropped the O's from second to fourth place with a 29–26 record, Williams made the move he had contemplated for a year. He lured Weaver back with a $1 million offer to manage through the rest of 1985 and for the entire 1986 season. But despite a career year from Mike Young (.273 average, 28 HRs, 81 RBIs) and monster years by Eddie Murray (.297, 31 HRs, 124 RBIs) and Cal Ripken (.282, 26 HRs, 110 RBIs), the Orioles' struggles continued. While they gained 18 games on the Tigers from the year before, they went only 53–52 under Weaver and remained in fourth place, 16 games behind the Toronto Blue Jays, who broke through to win their first divisional title.

If 1985 ranked as the biggest disappointment of Williams's tenure as club owner, then 1986 could only be described as a disaster. The season started innocently enough, with the team treading water through most of the first half. A week short of the first anniversary of Weaver's return, the Orioles were 33–20, in second place, just three games behind the Blue Jays, but as it turned out, that would be their high-water mark, 13 games over .500.

The next stretch of 20 games, 15 of them losses, was a sign of impending disaster, but as had happened so often in Weaver's career, the O's rebounded strongly. By August 5, they were back in second place, only two and a half games out, with a 59–47 record and seemingly poised for a big stretch run.

The next night Larry Sheets and Jim Dwyer hit grand-slam home runs—both in the fourth inning—as the Orioles momentarily enthralled a Memorial Stadium audience of 19,519 by overcoming an early 6–0 Texas lead. Two months later Dwyer would replay that moment in his mind, still unable to rationalize what eventually happened. "Right then, after those two homers, I said to myself, 'We're going to win it,'" he recalled. "I was sure of it."

As it developed, the Orioles wouldn't even win that game. The Rangers pounded out 19 hits en route to a 13–11 win. If ever one game seemed to demolish a season, it was that one. The game on August 6, 1986, not only set the tone for what remained of that season, but also for the rest of what turned out to be a disastrous mini-era. The Orioles would go 14–42 the rest of the way, a .250 winning percentage that capped the only losing season on Weaver's record, sending the colorful and immensely popular skipper into a final retirement.

It also marked the end of Rick Dempsey's initial eleven-year run in Baltimore. After the Orioles made a trade for veteran catcher Terry Kennedy, Dempsey opted for free agency and a chance to play regularly in Cleveland rather than accept a backup role. It would be another five years before he would return for a final cameo as a player and a stint as a coach before settling in for a long run in the TV booth.

Meanwhile, the Orioles' foray into the free-agent market was not producing many positive results. Don Aase set a then-club record with 34 saves as an All-Star reliever in 1986, but he was a nonfactor because of injuries the last two years of his

BELOW: Richie Bancells began as a minor league trainer for the Orioles in 1977, became Ralph Salvon's assistant in 1984, and in 1988 became only the third head athletic trainer in club history, a position he has held for 27 seasons.
BOTTOM: The first of two second-round picks by the Orioles in the 1978 draft (the other being Cal Ripken Jr.), Larry Sheets produced 17 and 18 homers in his first two full seasons in 1985 and 1986. In 1987 he was named Most Valuable Oriole after leading the team with a .318 average and 31 homers and finishing second to Ripken with 94 RBI. After hitting just 17 homers over the next two seasons, he was traded to the Tigers.

contract. Fred Lynn's numbers were amazingly consistent—he hit 23 home runs in each of his three full seasons in Baltimore but was never able to play more than 124 games.

The 1987 season presented Cal Ripken Sr., a career organizational man for the O's who had played and coached under Weaver, with the chance to take on his dream job: to be the Orioles' manager on a team that included two of his sons, Cal Jr. and Bill. Part of the coaching staff for the previous eleven years, Cal Sr. was aware of the pitfalls of managing, but it was the opportunity he yearned for. Indeed, managing his sons was the most satisfying experience of his long and loyal career.

In 1987, the Orioles added another free agent in addition to Kennedy—Ray Knight, one of the heroes of the Mets' 1986 World Series run. But the 1987 season gave O's fans little to cheer about, as the Orioles limped to a 67–95 record, their worst since the club's second season in 1955, and were outscored 880–729 in the process.

It didn't take long for Williams to make some moves. At the end of the season, calling the team's play over the previous two years "embarrassing," Williams dismissed General Manager Hank Peters and his top lieutenant, minor league director Tom Giordano. The Orioles had won two pennants and a World Series during their tenure, but Williams, who had health issues and was continuing to press the new stadium issue, was anxious to right the ship.

Veteran baseball executive Roland Hemond was brought in to replace Peters as general manager, while Doug Melvin, who had been brought in a year earlier, took over the minor league operation. Neither could have known that 1987 was only a mild preview of what was to come.

One week into what would be a memorably forgettable 1988 season, the Orioles did not have a win—and Cal Sr. didn't have a job. Hemond, still trying to get his feet grounded with a new team, made the move after only six games. With Edward William's encouragement, Hemond summoned Frank Robinson to be the new manager.

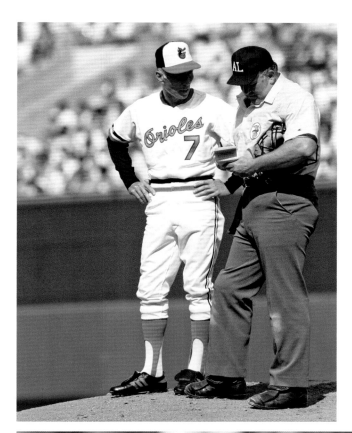

OPPOSITE TOP: The Rangers' Toby Harrah, flanked by the Orioles' Larry Sheets (left) and Jim Dwyer, poses after the trio combined for a record three grand slams on August 6, 1986. Sheets and Dwyer hit theirs during a nine-run fourth inning, but the Rangers came back to win, 13–11.

OPPOSITE BOTTOM: The son of former Oriole Bob Kennedy, Terry Kennedy made the 1987 AL All-Star team in the first of his two seasons as Orioles catcher, finishing the season with a .250 average, 18 homers, and 62 RBIs. The next season, as his average hovered below the .200 mark until mid-August, Kennedy ended up sharing the catching duties with Mickey Tettleton.

LEFT: Cal Ripken Sr. changes pitchers during the 1987 season, his only full season as manager. The rebuilding Orioles won just 67 games that year, and after an 0–6 start in '88, Ripken was replaced by Frank Robinson.

BELOW: More than "Cal's younger brother," Bill Ripken was a sure-handed second baseman whose hard-nosed play led to several trips to the disabled list during his time with the Orioles. Called up in July 1987, he batted .308 over the 58 games that season and led the team with a .291 batting average in 1990, but he never hit better than .239 in five other seasons with the Orioles. In a poll of AL managers in 1991, he was rated the second best defensive second baseman in the league, behind Toronto's Roberto Alomar.

O's PROFILE EDDIE MURRAY: STEADY EDDIE

From the stands the chants came often and loud, a vocal sign of reverence: "ED–DIE!! ED–DIE!!"

In the clubhouse, fellow players honored Eddie Murray in a more understated, and occasionally joking and irreverent, way. They referred to him by a nickname that embodied the kind of respect reserved for those who perform at the highest level: "Steady Eddie." If it's possible to encapsulate a Hall of Fame player in one word, his teammates had it right because "steady" best summarizes the career of Eddie Murray.

To fully understand his career, not only the thirteen years with the Orioles but the twenty-one years overall, one has to appreciate the value of consistency. Through his first nine years with the Orioles, Murray drove in fewer than 95 runs only twice—his first year in 1977, when he had 88 en route to Rookie of the Year honors, and the strike shortened 1981 season, when he led the American League with 78.

Five times in those first nine years he had over 100 RBIs, and over that stretch he hit between 22 and 33 home runs each year, with a batting average that never dropped below .283. He averaged 26 home runs and 94 RBIs for his thirteen years in an Orioles' uniform. Over his entire career, his numbers of 3,255 hits, 504 home runs, and 1,917 RBIs remain a lasting testimony to his remarkable consistency.

But as he pointed out during the ceremonies unveiling his statue in Legends Park at Camden Yards in 2012, Eddie Murray was not about statistics. He was about winning and playing the game right—and in his mind, one fed off the other. "It's all about teammates," said Murray. "You go out and put yourself on the line for each other, trying to win for each other, day in and day out.

"There's nothing better than winning. I wish we could have won more than one [World Series], but 1983 was the only one. Everybody always asks, 'What was that like, what was the most important thing?' Honestly, being in that room, laughing, smiling, pouring that champagne. . . . I mean, it was awesome."

When he was inducted into the National Baseball Hall of Fame on July 27, 2003, Murray elaborated on the sport's team aspect, which has defined the Orioles ever since the arrival of Frank Robinson and the first of the "Glory Years" in 1966. "Baseball is a team game," Murray said in 2003. "You win as a team, you lose as a team, and you also do so many things together. It's not an 'I' or 'me' thing. For me baseball is about the team winning. That's what I'm all about."

Along the way, Murray emulated his own role models, citing the influence Elrod Hendricks and Lee May had on him as a young player. "Elrod was special, he was like one of my head coaches," said Murray. "He caught on to what you were doing and fixed it if necessary, and then say you're doing pretty good. Lee, man, he was tough love . . . but what love. He was a tough guy. I loved him then and am still tight with his family."

During his 2003 Cooperstown speech, and again at the unveiling of his statue, Murray paid tribute to those who were most influential in his early days in the organization. "When I became a minor leaguer with the Orioles at the age of seventeen, I ran into my good friend's dad, Cal Ripken Sr. 'Old Man Rip' was a special man. If he loved you, that man would overwhelm you with knowledge of baseball. He was a tremendous baseball person, and he really meant a lot to me."

Murray credits Cal Sr. and Jim Schaffer, the Orioles' Class AA manager at Asheville in 1974, with helping him "make the most important decision in my career" to become a switch-hitter. One of the more remarkable aspects of Murray's legendary career is that he became a switch-hitter less than two years before coming to the big leagues.

Once he made it to spring training with the Orioles in 1977, there was no looking back. He opened the eyes of Manager Earl Weaver, who envisioned a star in the making, even if it was a year or two ahead of schedule. "I know Earl fought to keep me that year," said Murray. "He fought some battles to get me there, and I appreciate it—I got to play with Mr. [Brooks] Robinson. That clubhouse was unbelievable. It was a place you wanted to be. A place you learned to play the game. I couldn't have asked for better teammates. Those guys were all unbelievable to me."

In addition, Eddie also got to play for a manager who liked to write his name in the lineup every game, and it was a perfect matchup. "I'm proud to be here as the man who has played first base more than anybody in the game of baseball," Murray said during his Cooperstown induction speech. "It was never about taking days off for me. It was about showing up every day, letting my managers know that I was here to work. When I signed a contract, I was here to play 162 games. Earl didn't want to give me days off, and I liked that."

None of which was lost on the guy who would ultimately set the standard for daily performance. "Actually, Eddie was my role model for wanting to play every day," said Cal Ripken Jr., who would go on to set an all-time record by playing 2,632 consecutive games. "His approach was that it was important for him to be in the lineup. He knew he was counted on to be the number-four hitter, to be the man in the middle of the lineup. He knew the importance of being reliable."

For reasons that both sides probably thought were best, Murray was traded to the Dodgers after the club's disastrous 1988 season. As all would probably agree, it proved to be a mistake. Cal Jr. succinctly summed it up years later: "Eddie never should have left."

But, when the Orioles traded for Murray during the 1996 season, the two close friends paired up for a postseason run one last time. Ironically, Eddie would hit his 500th home run on September 6, 1996, exactly one year after Cal Jr. broke Lou Gehrig's record by playing in his 2,131st straight game. The Orioles would come up short of their World Series goal in 1996, but at least two of the organization's icons had a chance to reunite. Plus, the chants of "ED–DIE!! ED–DIE!!" allowed the fans and Murray to bring some closure to a mutually rewarding experience.

Like Cal Sr., Frank had long coveted the manager's job, and he probably understood that getting it was a matter of waiting his turn and paying his dues. He paid his dues, all right. The opening week losing streak didn't end; it kept going for an American League record 21 games—the Orioles would come within one game of going the entire month of April without a win.

Such futility didn't necessarily send shock waves through baseball, but it certainly confirmed that 1987 wasn't a fluke. And, in a year when almost nothing went right, even the season's first win was something of a disappointment.

The losing streak was at 12 when the Orioles embarked on a 12-game road trip that concluded in Chicago on May 1. As the losses kept piling up, the team developed a promotion designed to fill Memorial Stadium and send a message of hope and support when the team returned home on May 2. Fans rallied behind the idea, even though it would mean the O's would arrive winless for a month. However, the party to help break the streak was derailed when Mark Williamson and Dave Schmidt combined on a shutout to beat the White Sox 9–0 on April 29.

Two more losses followed, and on May 2, the 1-and-23 O's team was greeted by a raucous crowd of 50,402. Why the cheering? Before the game, owner Edward Williams had announced the team had signed a fifteen-year lease for a new downtown stadium. When Jay Tibbs and Doug Sisk combined on a six-hitter as the O's beat the Rangers, 9–4, halting their second losing streak at two, it was icing on the cake.

As the saying goes, the 1988 season was all downhill from there. It was also the end of another era, one that began with optimism and ended in despair. During this period, Mike Flanagan and Mike Boddicker, along with Fred Lynn, left in trades; Jim Palmer and Scott McGregor retired; and Rick Dempsey departed via free agency. A simmering feud also escalated between owner Edward Williams and Eddie Murray.

It was a period of high expectations, disappointments, anxiety, upheaval, turmoil, and the losingest two-year stretch in team history. And while it was a tougher stretch than Dempsey imagined as he pondered the future, sitting in front of his locker and basking in the glow of the 1983 World Series Championship trophy and his MVP award, it also precipitated a resurgence that was equally hard to predict.

TOP AND ABOVE: From the time he won the AL Rookie of the Year award in 1977, "Steady Eddie" Murray was the heart of the Orioles for more than a decade. As an Oriole, he batted .294 and hit 343 of his 504 career homers. One of only four players (along with Hank Aaron, Willie Mays, and Rafael Palmeiro) to collect 3,000 hits and 500 homers, Murray is the only player to collect 75 or more RBIs in each of his first 20 seasons, has more RBIs than any switch-hitter in history, and played more games and had more assists than any first baseman. He returned to the Orioles in a trade with the Indians in 1996 and on September 6 of that year hit his 500th career home run. He served as an Orioles coach from 1998 to 2001 and was elected to baseball's Hall of Fame on the first ballot in 2003.

MEMORABLE GAMES
1984–1988

May 6, 1984

Cal Ripken becomes the second Oriole to hit for the cycle, completing the feat with a ninth-inning home run in a 6–1 win at Texas' Arlington Stadium. After a first-inning flyout, Ripken triples in the third, singles in the fifth, doubles in the seventh, and hits a homer in his final at-bat to become the second Oriole to hit for the cycle, joining Brooks Robinson (Aubrey Huff and Felix Pie would later join them).

August 26, 1985

Eddie Murray hits three home runs at California and ties Jim Gentile's twenty-four-year-old club record with nine RBIs in a game. The Orioles match their club record with seven homers in a game, as John Shelby, Floyd Rayford, Gary Roenicke, and Rick Dempsey also go deep in the 17–3 win.

May 11, 1985

For the second straight night, Fred Lynn hits a ninth-inning homer to beat the Minnesota Twins. After leading off the ninth on May 10 with a homer off Ron Davis for a 6–5 win, Lynn comes to bat the next night in the ninth with two on and the O's trailing, 2–1. Twins manager Billy Gardner lifts Davis and brings in Curt Wardle, but Lynn greets him with a game-winning three-run homer before 49,094 fans at Memorial Stadium.

August 6, 1986

Jim Dwyer and Larry Sheets hit grand slams in the fourth inning, but it isn't enough as the Orioles fall to the Rangers, 13–11. Texas' Toby Harrah homers with the bases loaded in the second inning as the teams tie the AL record with three grand slams in the same game.

May 28, 1987

Mike Young homers in the 10th and 12th innings, the second a two-run shot to beat the Angels, 8–7, to become just the fifth player ever to hit two extra-inning home runs. The Orioles hit a Memorial Stadium club-record six home runs in the game (Larry Sheets hits two, and Cal Ripken and Rick Burleson add one each), and the Angels add two for another stadium record.

September 14, 1987

Orioles pitchers allow a major league-record 10 home runs in an 18–3 loss at Toronto, prompting Manager Cal Ripken Sr. to remove Cal Ripken Jr. from the game and end his consecutive innings streak at a record 8,243. He is replaced at shortstop by Ron Washington in the eighth inning.

July 11, 1987

Bill Ripken is called up from the minors, joining his brother Cal Jr. and his father Cal Sr. on the Orioles. It is the first time in major league history that two brothers are managed by their father. Bill starts at second base and Cal at shortstop, but the two combine to go 0-for-7 as the Orioles lose to Minnesota, 2–1.

May 2, 1988

Returning home with a 1–23 record—including a major league record 21-game losing streak to begin the season—the Orioles are greeted by 50,402 faithful on Fantastic Fans Night at Memorial Stadium. Prior to the game, Orioles owner Edward Bennett Williams and Maryland governor William Donald Schaefer announce that they have reached agreement to build a new ballpark for the Orioles. The Orioles go on to a 9–4 win over the Rangers.

CHAPTER 10

SAYING GOOD-BYE TO THE OLD GREY LADY

As they prepared for the final chapter of the tumultuous 1980s, the Orioles were clearly in uncharted territory and facing a series of dramatic changes. Their magnificent twenty-year run of success had been relegated to the past tense, replaced by feelings of uncertainty as the team prepared for the transition from Memorial Stadium to Camden Yards.

Late-season ventures into the trade market in '87 and '88 led to the departure of veterans Fred Lynn, Mike Flanagan, and Mike Boddicker, while bringing in Brady Anderson, Curt Schilling, Chris Hoiles, and Jose Mesa. But it would take time for the makeover to take effect. When Edward Bennett Williams passed away August 13, 1988, five months after signing the lease for a new downtown baseball park, it left an ownership void that wasn't resolved until December 6, when a group headed by Eli Jacobs bought the team for $70 million.

Ironically, the new ownership finalized the deal two days after a trade that sent Eddie Murray, who had fallen into disfavor with previous ownership, to the Dodgers in exchange for pitchers Brian Holton and Ken Howell and shortstop Juan Bell. The change in ownership was formally approved April 18, 1989, shortly after the start of the most improbable season in the Orioles' history.

The bitter taste of 1988's 54–107 record left little reason to expect more than modest improvement in 1989, despite the addition of young players like Steve Finley, Bob Milacki, and Gregg Olson, and the emergence of Jeff Ballard as an effective top-of-the-rotation starter. The trade of Murray left Cal Ripken Jr. as the unquestioned face of the franchise, and it also led to Ripkin's short-lived experiment at third base.

Prior to the 1989 season, Juan Bell was anointed the heir apparent at shortstop. Manager Frank Robinson determined that a firm decision needed to be made no

OPPOSITE: The final walk. Mike Flanagan wanted to be the last Oriole to throw a pitch at Memorial Stadium when he returned to the club as a left-handed relief specialist in 1991. He got his wish in the final game on October 6, 1991, striking out both Tiger batters he faced.

> **"** As the season neared the halfway point, optimism swelled, and whenever someone asked Frank Robinson why he thought the Orioles could win the division, he fell into the habit of answering the question with his own question. 'Why not?'"

later than mid-March, giving the team two weeks to readjust if necessary. After looking at the new alignment for three weeks in spring training, Robinson made the decision to move Ripken back to shortstop, where he would stay for eight more years. Bell, meanwhile, spent most of the next two years in the minors, getting only six at-bats with the Orioles.

The Orioles were a unanimous choice to finish last in the American League's Eastern Division in 1989, and their 14–15 record in spring training did little to convince anyone that they would contend. With an average age of 26.1 years, they were the youngest team in baseball.

Nevertheless, as the season headed into the second month, it was obvious this was a far different team than the one that finished 1988. And as the season neared the halfway point, optimism swelled, and whenever someone asked Frank Robinson why he thought the Orioles could win the division, he fell into the habit of answering the question with his own question.

"Why not?" he replied each time. This standard reply became the team's rallying cry, which was repeated and heard until the next to last day of the season. The rest of the division wasn't exactly setting a fast pace. For instance, even though the Orioles lost 17 of their first 30 games, they moved into first place with a 22–21 record following a 5–2 win at Cleveland on May 26, 1989.

Incredibly, despite losing 12 of 13 at one point in August, the Orioles maintained at least a share of first place until September 1, when a 10–1 loss to the White Sox dropped them into second place for good. However, the Orioles remained in contention until the next to last day of the season, which led to a final weekend showdown in Toronto so dramatic that it completely overshadowed the first matchup of teams led by black managers—Frank Robinson and the Blue Jays' Cito Gaston.

Trailing by one game, the Orioles needed to sweep the three-game series to clinch the division or win two to force a one-game playoff in Baltimore the day after the regular season ended. Phil Bradley tried to set the tone early, hitting the first pitch of the first game into the left-field seats, but it proved to be the Orioles' only run in perhaps their most gut-wrenching loss of the year.

In the eighth inning, the score was still 1–0, but Toronto had a runner on first and one out. American League Rookie of the Year Gregg Olson relieved Jeff Ballard. After a stolen base and a ground out moved the runner to third base, Olson bounced a curveball that got away from catcher Jamie Quirk, allowing the tying run to score. "Jamie wanted to 'man up' and take the blame," Olson said later, "but he really had no chance."

Olson struck out Kelly Gruber to end that inning, and he pitched two more scoreless innings before the Blue Jays pushed across a run in the 11th for a 2–1 win that assured them no worse than a tie for the division title.

There was no letup in the drama the next day—either on the field or in the front office. Pete Harnisch, the Orioles' scheduled starter, suffered a freak injury the night before when he stepped on a nail while walking back to the hotel. Dave Johnson, pitching on three days' rest, got the start instead and nursed a 3–1 lead into the eighth inning, when things unraveled.

Johnson was pulled after a leadoff walk to Nelson Liriano. Then pitcher Kevin Hickey walked Manny Lee, and new pitcher Mark Williamson allowed a sacrifice bunt, a couple of singles, and a sacrifice fly. For the second straight game, the Blue Jays managed a comeback win, this one 4–3, and clinched the division title. This ended General Manager Roland Hemond's plan for a super-surprise ending for the last day of the regular season.

OPPOSITE TOP: The number one overall pick in the 1989 first-year player draft after being named college player of the year at LSU, Ben McDonald made his big league debut less than three weeks after signing with the Orioles. He went 58–53 with a 3.89 ERA in seven seasons with the Birds.
OPPOSITE BOTTOM: Mickey Tettleton became a cult hero during his three years as Orioles catcher, 1988–1990, when it was said he derived his power from eating Fruit Loops cereal every morning.
TOP LEFT: In four seasons with the Orioles, Randy Milligan would serve as the primary first baseman during the 1989 "Why Not?" season and appear in 137 games in the inaugural season of Camden Yards.
TOP RIGHT: Storm Davis, who went 54–40 as a starter from 1982 to 1986, returned in 1992 as a reliever and went 7–3.
ABOVE: Bob Melvin, later a two-time Manager of the Year in the majors, platooned at catcher for the Orioles from 1989 to 1991, batting .244.

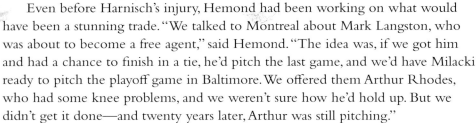

Even before Harnisch's injury, Hemond had been working on what would have been a stunning trade. "We talked to Montreal about Mark Langston, who was about to become a free agent," said Hemond. "The idea was, if we got him and had a chance to finish in a tie, he'd pitch the last game, and we'd have Milacki ready to pitch the playoff game in Baltimore. We offered them Arthur Rhodes, who had some knee problems, and we weren't sure how he'd hold up. But we didn't get it done—and twenty years later, Arthur was still pitching."

Yet another close call for a season that started with a question that led to a slogan. Coming on the heels of the worst back-to-back seasons in franchise history, "Why Not?" became a rallying cry heading into the next decade.

It wasn't like the Orioles had a lot of players coming off career years in what appeared to be a breakout season. Phil Bradley's .277 average was the best among the regulars, Cal Ripken (93 RBIs) was the only player with more RBIs than rookie Craig Worthington's 70 RBIs, and although Ballard's 18–8 record was among the league's best, the team's 4.00 ERA was a mediocre ninth-best in the league.

Unfortunately, the newfound optimism didn't have much staying power. "Why Not?" quickly became "How Come?" as the Orioles struggled for consistency in 1990. They flirted with the .500 mark a few times, but never rose above that break-even point after April 23. Ballard inexplicably saw his record fall to 2–11, Milacki's record dropped to 5–8 (down from 14–12 in 1989). Johnson (13–11) emerged as the most consistent starter, but there was a noticeable offensive decline. Bill Ripken led the team with a .291 average, while Cal's modest 21 home runs and 84 RBIs were indicative of the team's overall drop in run production (708–669).

That offensive decline played a big role in an off-season trade that dramatically affected the club's immediate future. In an effort to bulk up the lineup, the Orioles traded three young prospects—Pete Harnisch, Steve Finley, and Curt Schilling—to Houston for Glenn Davis, a first baseman with proven power.

The trade was met with mostly favorable reactions at the time. But Davis immediately broke down with injuries—in total over the next three years, he had only 687 at-bats, and his overall home run (24) and RBI (85) totals were less than his single-season projections. It quickly became obvious that the trade had set the Orioles back, and the 1991 season turned into a disaster that cost Manager Frank Robinson his job. Midseason, first-base coach Johnny Oates took over the team,

ABOVE LEFT: The Orioles take the field for the last game at Memorial Stadium: (From left to right) Bob Milacki, Glenn Davis, Leo Gomez, Bob Melvin, Cal Ripken, Dwight Evans, Bill Ripken, Joe Orsulak, and (not seen) Mike Devereaux.
ABOVE: Doug DeCinces (left) and the legend he replaced at third, Brooks Robinson, together again for the final game at Memorial Stadium, October 6, 1971.
OPPOSITE TOP: Pitchers spanning thirty-eight years of Orioles memories take the mound during post-game ceremonies following the last game at Memorial Stadium on October 6, 1991.
OPPOSITE BOTTOM LEFT: Rick Dempsey leads one last "O-R-I-O-L-E-S" cheer at Memorial Stadium.
OPPOSITE BOTTOM RIGHT: Dennis Martinez, the first Nicaraguan-born player in the majors, waves to the crowd after the final game at Memorial Stadium. Martinez, the winningest Latin pitcher in big league history, won the first 108 of his 245 victories with the Orioles from 1976 to 1986.
FOLLOWING PAGES: More than one-hundred current and former Oriole players, coaches, and managers were on hand for the final game at Memorial Stadium, taking part in postgame ceremonies to close "the Grey Lady of 33rd Street."

TOP LEFT: Joe Orsulak spent five seasons with the Orioles, leading the team with a .288 average in his first season in 1988 and .289 in his final season in 1992. In 1991 he led the majors with 22 outfield assists, an Orioles record.
TOP RIGHT: Colts quarterback John Unitas (left) and Orioles third baseman Brooks Robinson threw out the first balls prior to the final Orioles game at Memorial Stadium.
ABOVE MIDDLE: (From left to right) Bob Milacki, Mike Flanagan, Mark Williamson, and Gregg Olson became the first quartet in big league history to combine on a no-hitter when they beat the A's, 2–0, on July 13, 1991.
ABOVE: Gregg Olson, the Orioles' number-one pick in the 1988 draft went on to become the first reliever to be named AL Rookie of the Year in 1989.

which limped to a 67–95 record and a sixth-place finish, 24 games behind the Blue Jays. What had been billed as "A Season to Remember," to commemorate the last year played in Memorial Stadium, quickly became one to forget.

The bitter disappointment over the season clouded two positive developments: Cal Ripken won his second Most Valuable Player Award (hitting .323, 34 HRs, and 114 RBIs), and pitching prospect Mike Mussina emerged to show promise late in the season.

As the season wound down, the only thing fans looked forward to was the final weekend, a three-game series against the Detroit Tigers that would be used to celebrate Memorial Stadium and rekindle fond memories of the past. Anticipation grew about how the Orioles would handle ceremonies, and those plans remained guarded until the very end, when 50,700 people crammed into the thirty-eight-year-old stadium that had played such a prominent role in Baltimore's major league baseball and football history. The final game itself was an afterthought, the result meaningless, the crowd impatient for the postgame festivities.

Everybody knew Manager Johnny Oates had a game plan for the ninth inning. Regardless of circumstances, ace closer Gregg Olson would start the ninth inning, and Mike Flanagan, once a Cy Young Award–winning starter, now a relief specialist, would be called on to get the last out. But after getting one out, Olson called Oates out of the dugout and altered the plan.

"These people don't want to see me—they want Flanny," Olson told the manager, who quickly obliged. Flanagan admitted his walk from the bullpen was deliberately slow. "I was thinking of all the guys who had pitched on that mound and felt like they were going out there with me," he said. Flanagan then ended the inning with a pair of strikeouts, providing the game's home team highlight. It then remained for Tigers' pitcher Frank Tanana to finish off a masterful performance in a 7–1 victory, getting Cal Ripken to ground into a game-ending double play as the last at-bat ever at Memorial Stadium. Tanana celebrated by waving his cap in a salute to the fans, acknowledging the standing-room-only crowds that had filled the old park all weekend.

After the teams left the field, the drama gradually unfolded. Members of the grounds crew, suitably dressed in tuxedos, emerged from a limousine to dig up home plate and transport it to the new field, Camden Yards, where it would be planted in place.

And then, with music from the film *Field of Dreams* playing, the parade began. First came Brooks Robinson, trotting to third base, where he revived his ritual of pawing at the dirt as the crowd erupted, beginning a roar that remained constant for the better part of an hour. Next came Frank Robinson, the last man to touch home plate before continuing to his position in right field.

Fittingly, Carl Ripken Jr. was the last player to take the field—leaving former manager Earl Weaver to make the final entrance, with tears flowing freely as the crowd's continuous roar reached a crescendo."

Boog Powell was next, taking up his post at first base. There was no mistaking the sound of the "g" as the long "Booooooog" chants rang out. Jim Palmer darted to the pitching mound—exactly twenty-five years to the day since he beat Sandy Koufax, 6–0, in Game 2 of the 1966 World Series. That happened in Dodger Stadium, and now he was on the pitching mound at Memorial Stadium for the last time. When a closeup camera shot revealed the tears in his eyes, it seemed like everyone lost it.

"The players were watching the TV in the clubhouse," Oates revealed later, "and there was some laughter when they showed a little old lady crying. Then they saw Palmer, and all of sudden there wasn't a sound."

As the steady stream of players from the past came from the dugout and went to their positions, no introductions were necessary. Everybody knew who they were. At one point Palmer, Dave McNally, Mike Cuellar, and Pat Dobson, the quartet of 20-game winners from 1971, were alone on the pitching mound.

One by one, they kept coming—except when John Lowenstein and Gary Roenicke went to left field together, a fitting entry for the famed platoon pairing. Bob Turley, who threw the first pitch in 1954, was there. So were Hall of Famers Robin Roberts and Luis Aparicio. Paulie Blair was in centerfield, the Blade (Mark Belanger) at shortstop, and Bobby Grich at second base.

Some were stars, some were substitutes with a special bond. Dennis Martinez, who had pitched a perfect game for the Montreal Expos that year, got a special pass so he could attend. So did Rick Dempsey, who was allowed to miss Milwaukee's last game.

On this day, everybody was a star. When infielder Lenn Sakata trotted out to take his place with the catchers, everybody knew why—that's where he was the day Tippy Martinez picked three runners off first base, just before the emergency catcher hit a three-run homer to win the game.

Eighty former Orioles took their positions before the 1991 team made its entrance. "For many of them, I think it was the first time they realized the history of the Orioles," said Oates, an observation later confirmed by several players.

Fittingly, Carl Ripken Jr. was the last player to take the field—leaving former manager Earl Weaver to make the final entrance, with tears flowing freely as the crowd's continuous roar reached a crescendo. As the video board showed home plate being put in place at Camden Yards, and with the *Field of Dreams* music still playing, everyone in uniform assembled in a circle around the pitching mound for one last group picture.

It then remained for Dempsey to perform his patented O–R–I–O–L–E–S routine, contorting his body to spell out the letters one last time. From the final out to the final roar, the only sounds came from the music and the cheers. Words would have been inadequate.

Memorial Stadium's glorious era was over, but not soon to be forgotten.

TOP: (From left to right) Shortstop and Coach Bill Hunter, Manager Earl Weaver, Coach and Manager Cal Ripken Sr., and Manager Billy Hitchcock pose during ceremonies after the last Orioles game at Memorial Stadium. ABOVE: Johnny Oates is one of two men to play for, coach, and manage the Orioles. He replaced Frank Robinson, the only other person to do it all, on May 23, 1991.

MEMORABLE GAMES
1989–1991

April 3, 1989

The Orioles open the season with a 5–4 win over Boston at Memorial Stadium. Cal Ripken's three-run homer off Red Sox ace Roger Clemens gives the O's a sixth-inning lead, but it is Craig Worthington's single in the 11th inning that is the game-winner.

July 15, 1989

Is it fair or foul? Trailing the Angels, 9–7, in the last of the ninth inning, the Orioles score twice before Mike Devereaux pulls a two-run homer down the left field line for an 11–9 win to send 47,393 Orioles fans into delirious delight. The entire Angels team besieges the umpires, claiming the ball curved foul before reaching the bleachers. The home run stands.

May 20, 1989

Jeff Ballard improves his record to 7–1 with a 5–1 win over Cleveland as the Orioles tie the Indians and move within a half game of first-place Boston. Ballard works into the eighth inning and Gregg Olson strikes out two batters over the final inning and a third, as the upstart Birds begin to wonder, "Why not?"

September 30, 1989

After winning only 54 games the previous season, the Orioles battle Toronto into the final weekend for the AL East crown. In the next-to-last game of the season, Dave Johnson—a last-second fill-in starter— allows only two runs over seven innings, but the bullpen can't hold the lead and the Orioles fall, 4–3, at the Skydome, giving the Blue Jays the title.

July 13, 1991

Four Oriole pitchers combine to no-hit the A's at the Oakland Coliseum, the Birds' only no-hitter on the road. Bob Milacki goes six innings, and Mike Flanagan, Mark Williamson, and Gregg Olson each throw an inning of no-hit ball as the O's win, 2–0.

June 12, 1990

The Orioles beat Milwaukee, 4–3, in 10 innings, as the Brewers' Dan Plesac gives up a two-out game-tying homer to Mickey Tettleton in the ninth and a lead-off homer to Randy Milligan in the 10th. Shortstop Cal Ripken plays in his 1,308th consecutive game, moving past Everett Scott for the second-longest streak of all time and the longest at one position. (Lou Gehrig's longest streak was 885 games at first base.)

October 6, 1991

After thirty-eight years, the Orioles play their final game ever at Memorial Stadium, losing to the Tigers, 7–1. Mike Flanagan fulfills his wish as he comes in from the bullpen and strikes out the final two Detroit batters to become the last Oriole to throw a pitch on 33rd Street. Then more than a hundred former and current Orioles take the field for a stirring farewell to the stadium.

CHAPTER 11

THE BALLPARK THAT FOREVER CHANGED BASEBALL

When the team began razing the 85 acres of land that would eventually house Oriole Park at Camden Yards on June 28, 1989, nobody dreamed it was the first step toward building the "Ballpark that Forever Changed Baseball." It just happened.

Even when construction started a little more than seven months later, on February 6, 1990, debate centered on whether the iconic B&O Warehouse should stay or go or what the historic venture should be named. Few discussed what kind of impact a new downtown, baseball-only facility would have, not only for Baltimore and the Orioles, but for Major League Baseball in general.

The site certainly has history. It was once a train station for the Baltimore and Ohio Railroad, where Abraham Lincoln apparently put the finishing touches on the Gettysburg Address. It is also a mere two blocks from the birthplace of Babe Ruth, one of the game's most iconic figures (the site is now a museum). Ruth's Cafe, owned by Babe's father, once sat where center field is positioned. Only a few blocks away is the Inner Harbor, whose refurbishment a decade earlier had signaled a rebirth of Baltimore's downtown area.

Club owner Eli Jacobs was in favor of calling the stadium "Oriole Park," a name widely used throughout the city's previous major and minor league days, while Governor William Donald Schaefer championed "Camden Yards" as the official title. It wasn't until the final weekend at Memorial Stadium in 1991 that the compromise of "Oriole Park at Camden Yards" was officially adopted.

No baseball-only facilities had been built since Kansas City's Royal (now Kauffman) Stadium was built in 1973, yet two opened within a year of each other. The first was the new Comiskey Park in Chicago, which opened in April 1991; Camden Yards followed the next spring. Ironically, the Kansas City architectural firm HOK designed both the new Comiskey Park and Baltimore's Camden Yards. The project also received input from the Orioles and the state of Maryland, which owns and operates the building under the guidance of the Maryland Stadium Authority.

OPPOSITE: Twilight action in 2013.
FOLLOWING PAGES: Oriole Park at Camden Yards was called "the ballpark that forever changed baseball" after it opened in 1992.

The original design submitted by HOK was similar to the one in Chicago, but it was quickly rejected. With the urban design firm RTKL working under contract with HOK, a new look began to evolve that set the standard for decades. The finished project was, and is, an urban blend that reflects downtown Baltimore and gives fans an experience reminiscent of parks from the early twentieth century. Using steel rather than concrete and with a red brick façade that fits into the neighborhood, the park recalls some of the great ballparks of the past. The original design has a retro feel that incorporates the old B&O Warehouse as a signature feature, when some had feared that building would become an eyesore. The project took thirty-three months to complete, from razing buildings to completing the construction.

The playing field is asymmetrical, like most fields were in the early eras of baseball, presenting different challenges in all three outfield positions. It is also 16 feet below street level, which brings the right-field pavilion close to the scene and adds the spectacle of "Eutaw Street home runs," which reach the vendor areas. The Warehouse, now used as offices by the Orioles and several other firms, dominates the skyline around Camden Yards, with an appearance of being so close, yet so far away.

The anticipation of the opening of downtown Baltimore's newest addition rivaled the celebration that surrounded the closing of Memorial Stadium. As the ballpark took shape and fans got a glimpse of what was taking place, it became apparent that something special was going to unfold. Camden Yards didn't disappoint. After playing an exhibition game against the Mets two days before the official opening, Cal Ripken Jr. probably summed up the aura of the new ballpark best. "You get the feeling this wasn't the first game played here," said the future Hall of Fame shortstop.

When the park opened officially on April 6, 1992, Oriole Park at Camden Yards was dubbed "an instant classic." It was brand-new but old-fashioned, modern and retro at the same time. Ideas were borrowed, but nothing was copied, from some of the great ballparks of the past, and a trend had been set, a path created for other teams and cities to follow.

Even while under construction, Oriole Park at Camden Yards became a favorite topic of conversation in baseball circles—so much so that the 1993 All-Star Game was awarded to Baltimore well before the stadium was completed. Then, during the Home Run Derby the day before the 1993 All-Star contest, Ken Griffey Jr. became the first player to hit a ball off the Warehouse. Twenty-two years later, despite the relative proximity (439 feet at its closest spot), the Warehouse remains untouched in a regulation game. The club-level seats in left field—which Juan Gonzalez reached during the same contest—have proven to be almost as formidable, with only two home runs (by Rex Hudler and Mark Reynolds) having reached that area.

THESE PAGES: Camden Yards during construction in February 1992.

Not unexpectedly, the new ballpark proved to be an instant hit at the turnstiles. From May 23, 1992, through April 20, 1993, the Orioles had a streak of 65 straight sellouts, a record that would last until Cleveland, playing in new Jacobs Field (in many ways a replica of Camden Yards), presold all of its games in 1996 to break the record. In the strike-shortened 1995 season, the Orioles drew 3,098,475 spectators to lead the American League in attendance for the first time in club history, a feat they would duplicate the next three years.

During their first twenty-two years at Camden Yards, the Orioles drew a total of 60,345,788 spectators, or an average of 34,781 per home game. Over thirty-eight years in Memorial Stadium, they drew 49,845,588, or an average of 18,353 per date. After drawing 2 million in a season twice at Memorial Stadium, the Orioles have topped that mark eighteen times at Camden Yards, where the lowest yearly attendance of 1,733,019 in 2010 would've been the tenth highest at their former home.

Over the years, Camden Yards has aged gracefully, though there have been several subtle changes over the years. The most dramatic occurred in 2012, when the Orioles celebrated the park's twenty-year anniversary with a year-long celebration, highlighted by the unveiling of bronze sculptures of the team's six Hall of Fame members—Brooks Robinson, Frank Robinson, Jim Palmer, Earl Weaver, Eddie Murray, and Cal Ripken Jr. The sculptures occupy the area beyond the left-field bullpens, and it remains a popular destination for visitors.

The twenty-year "makeover" also included the addition of a fan-friendly lounge area above the "batter's eye" wall above the center-field fence, and the seating capacity was reduced from its original 48,290 to 45,971 with wider seats to provide additional comfort.

Twenty-two years later, Oriole Park at Camden Yards is now the eighth oldest ballpark in America, but in many aspects it remains the most treasured of them all. Of the twenty-one ballparks that have since been built or totally made over (as was the Angels stadium in Anaheim), most copied some aspects of Oriole Park at Camden Yards.

But "the Ballpark that Forever Changed Baseball" won't be duplicated.

LEFT: Opening Day 2012 at Camden Yards. The scoreboard shows a tribute to Earl Weaver, the Hall of Fame manager who had passed away ten weeks earlier.
FOLLOWING PAGES: The home plate façade at Oriole Park at Camden Yards during the 2012 season, twenty years after its opening.

CHAPTER 12

2131 AND A
WIRE-TO-WIRE RUN

Even before the good-bye celebration of Memorial Stadium was over, Orioles' manager Johnny Oates was planning to use the new park at Camden Yards as a recruiting tool. Oates was monitoring the comeback effort of Rick Sutcliffe, a former teammate with the Dodgers whose career was winding down.

A former Rookie of the Year and Cy Young Award winner, Sutcliffe was considering an offer to join his hometown Kansas City Royals, when Oates invited him to visit Baltimore, during which the pair just happened to drive past the nearly completed ballpark. "You're going to pitch the first game here," Oates said to Sutcliffe. Oates also hoped the veteran would be a good influence on his two young aces, Mike Mussina and Ben McDonald.

Oates's scheme worked, and as promised, Sutcliffe was on the mound when Oriole Park at Camden Yards opened on April 6, 1992. Then Sutcliffe created the sort of experience his new manager had hoped for. Sutcliffe not only pitched the first game, he also logged three other historical "firsts" for the new park: a win, a complete game, and a shutout. Behind their new pitcher, the Orioles blanked the Cleveland Indians, 2–0, before a sellout crowd of 44,568.

"This is the type of game we got Rick Sutcliffe to pitch," Oates said after the smashing debut. The impact of starting such a significant game wasn't lost on Sutcliffe. It gave him the perfect bookend for a previous historical appearance— August 8, 1988, when he was the Cubs' starting pitcher in the first night game ever played at Wrigley Field.

Sutcliffe delivered as promised in other ways during that inaugural season, going 16–15 and compiling 237 innings while serving as mentor to Mussina (18–5) and McDonald (13–13). As a result, the Orioles rebounded from a disastrous 67–95 record in 1991 and finished with a more-than-respectable 89–73 record in 1992,

OPPOSITE: On September 6, 1995, with the Orioles leading the Angels 3–1 in the middle of the fifth inning, the game became official, the numbers on the warehouse dropped, and Cal Ripken Jr. surpassed the immortal Lou Gehrig while playing in his 2,131st consecutive game, most in major league history. Ripken ended his streak voluntarily on September 20, 1998, sitting out the Orioles' last home game of the season after starting 2,632 straight games.

ABOVE: Orioles owner Peter Angelos bought the club in 1993 and has owned it longer than anyone in club history.

RIGHT: Rick Sutcliffe brought a veteran presence to the Orioles when he signed with the team before the 1992 season. He went 26–25 in two seasons as a starter. As the opening day starter at brand new Oriole Park at Camden Yards, he tossed a five-hit shutout to beat the Indians and went on to post a 16–15 record that year.

BELOW: One of three minor leaguers acquired from the Tigers late in the 1988 season for outfielder Fred Lynn, Chris Hoiles became the Orioles starting catcher in 1991 and finished his ten-year career second on the club in games caught and with more homers (151) than any other catcher. He was the Most Valuable Oriole in 1993 when he set career highs with a .310 average, 29 homers, and 82 RBIs. In 1992, he became the only player in big league history to hit at least 20 homers while driving in 40 or fewer runs.

good for a tie for third place in the AL East. But, as it turned out, the opening of Oriole Park at Camden Yards did more than signal the start of a new era in club history. It set the stage for a series of events that affected the organization's future.

The next year, the success of the 1993 All-Star Game, which introduced a weeklong "Fan Fest" celebration, had a lasting effect on the future of the midseason classic, just as the park itself had a dramatic influence on the other baseball venues built over the next two decades. But there was much more on the table during the second year at Oriole Park at Camden Yards.

Owner Eli Jacobs had been involved in protracted bankruptcy proceedings, and it became obvious the team would be sold, marking the team's fourth change of ownership. In mid-1993, it appeared the team would remain in control of out-of-town owners, as a group headed by Bill DeWitt (son of the man who traded Frank Robinson from Cincinnati to Baltimore) was on the verge of completing a deal. Then Baltimore attorney Peter Angelos spearheaded a local contingent that forced the sale to auction.

On August 2, 1993, less than a month after the spectacular success of the All-Star Game, the group of investors led by Angelos bought the team for $173 million; the sale was formally approved by American League owners on October 4, shortly after the Orioles completed an 85–77 season that tied them with the Tigers for third place in the AL East, albeit 10 games behind the eventual World Champion Blue Jays.

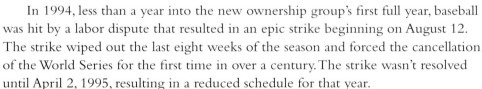

In 1994, less than a year into the new ownership group's first full year, baseball was hit by a labor dispute that resulted in an epic strike beginning on August 12. The strike wiped out the last eight weeks of the season and forced the cancellation of the World Series for the first time in over a century. The strike wasn't resolved until April 2, 1995, resulting in a reduced schedule for that year.

In between the two strike-shortened seasons, Phil Regan replaced Johnny Oates as manager of the Orioles. The team, handicapped by 1995's shortened spring training, struggled throughout the season and finished with a 71–73 record. Nevertheless, the Orioles drew 3,098,475 fans to lead the American League in attendance for the first time in history. The season was also salvaged by Cal Ripken Jr.'s historic run at Lou Gehrig's record of 2,130 consecutive games played. Finally, on September 6, 1995, the moment arrived. In a game witnessed by Hall of Famers Joe DiMaggio and Hank Aaron, and by President Bill Clinton and Vice President Al Gore (the first time a sitting president and vice president had attended the same game outside of Washington), Ripken broke Gehrig's record by playing in his 2,131st straight game. As an exclamation point, Ripken hit a home run (as he had the night before while tying the record), and this induced a forty-five-minute standing ovation that featured a celebratory lap around the field by the future Hall of Famer.

In 1996, the Orioles returned to postseason play for the first time in thirteen seasons. Davey Johnson replaced Regan as manager, and Pat Gillick joined the

TOP LEFT: Brady Anderson spent 14 of his 15 big league seasons with the Orioles and was the first player in AL history with 20 homers, 50 steals, and 75 RBIs in one season (1992). He hit 50 home runs in 1996 and was a three-time All-Star.

TOP RIGHT: A native of St. Michaels, Maryland, Harold Baines played in seven seasons over three different stints with the Orioles, compiling a .301 batting average and helping the team reach the postseason in 1996 and 1997.

ABOVE: Signed as a free agent after the '96 season, Mike Bordick took over shortstop (with Cal Ripken moving to third base) for the next three and a half years. After making the All-Star team in 2000, he was traded to the Mets in July, but he returned after the season as a free agent for two more seasons, setting AL records for a shortstop in 2002 for fewest errors (1), consecutive errorless games (110), and consecutive errorless chances (543).

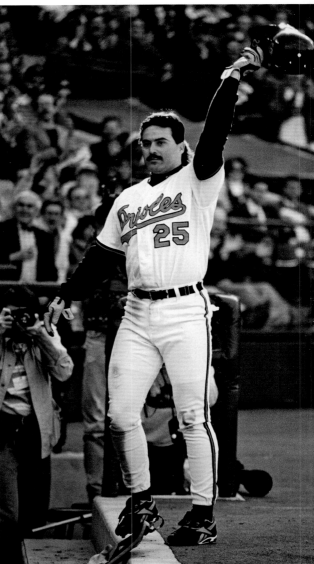

team as general manager. The Orioles were active in both the free-agent and trade markets, and the infusion of talented veterans paid off immediately. One highlight of the year was when Eddie Murray—brought back to Baltimore that year in a trade with Cleveland in July—hit his 500th home run one year to the day after Ripken broke Gehrig's record.

In 1996, the Orioles set a major league record with 10 players hitting 10 or more home runs. Brady Anderson hit 50 homers, breaking Frank Robinson's thirty-year-old club record, and Rafael Palmeiro added 39. Newly signed free agent Roberto Alomar batted .328 and scored a club-record 132 runs, and the Orioles scored the staggering total of 949 runs. The production was enough to offset an uncharacteristically high 5.41 team ERA. Working out of the bullpen, Arthur Rhodes had a 9–1 record in 28 games, and another new free agent, Randy Myers, converted 31 saves. Ultimately, the Orioles went 88–74 to claim the AL wild card spot (baseball had introduced the wild card to the playoffs in 1994). They won the best-of-five Division Series, beating Cleveland in four games. However, the 1996 ALCS with the Yankees got off to a bad start—in the eighth inning of Game 1, Derek Jeter hit a long fly ball that a fan, twelve-year-old Jeffrey Maier, attempted to catch, pulling the ball into the stands. Controversially, the umpires ruled the shot a home run, which tied the game, and the Orioles lost in extra innings. The Yankees eventually won the series in five games.

In 1997, fortified again by a veteran lineup, the Orioles left little doubt about the AL East title. The O's led the division wire-to-wire and posted a 98–74 record, despite the fact that their offensive output dropped by 137 runs to 812. Palmeiro had another strong year, with 38 home runs and 110 RBIs, and Robbie Alomar led the club with a .333 average. The pitching, meanwhile, recovered nicely and allowed only 681 runs (compared to 903 the year before) as Mike Mussina (15–8, 3.20 ERA), Scott Erickson (16–7, 3.69 ERA), and Jimmy Key (16–10, 3.43 ERA) led the way to the first divisional title since 1983.

As they had done the year before, the Orioles breezed through the Division Series, beating the Seattle Mariners in four games, but they came up short again in the ALCS, losing in six games to the Cleveland Indians, who won the last game, 1–0, on an 11th-inning home run by Tony Fernandez.

For the Baltimore Orioles, a heavily veteran team had put together two solid years, falling just short of the World Series each time. It was a good run, but 1997 proved to be the last gasp, and it would take awhile for the Orioles to recover.

OPPOSITE TOP LEFT: Eddie Murray acknowledges the crowd at Camden Yards after hitting his 500th career home run on September 6, 1996.

OPPOSITE TOP RIGHT: One of four men in history to get 3,000 hits and 500 home runs, Rafael Palmeiro will always be marked by his suspension for use of a banned substance during his second stint with the Orioles in 2005. In his first stint, from 1993 to 1997, Palmeiro led the Orioles in RBIs each year and in homers four times, averaging .292, 36 HRs, and 110 RBIs and twice winning a Gold Glove at first base.

OPPOSITE BOTTOM: Mike "Moose" Mussina spent the first 10 seasons of his career with the Orioles, from 1991 to 2000, and led the club in ERA eight times and in victories six times, going 147–81 with a 3.53 ERA. In the 1997 ALCS against Cleveland, "Moose" pitched 15 innings over two starts, allowing one run on four hits and four walks, but incredibly did not get a decision in either game.

TOP: Roberto Alomar spent three of his 16 Hall of Fame seasons as the Orioles' second baseman, from 1996 to 1998. He won two Gold Gloves and is the club's all-time leading hitter with a .312 average.

MIDDLE: Randy Myers earned 76 saves in two seasons as the Orioles closer in 1996–97. In '97, he led the league with 45 saves—including his last 34 straight—and had a career-best 1.51 ERA.

RIGHT: A former No. 1 overall draft pick by the Brewers, B.J. Surhoff joined the Orioles as a free agent in 1996 and became a versatile player and clutch hitter in two stints totaling eight seasons with the club. He batted .291 with 120 homers while starting at first and third base and left and right field at different times.

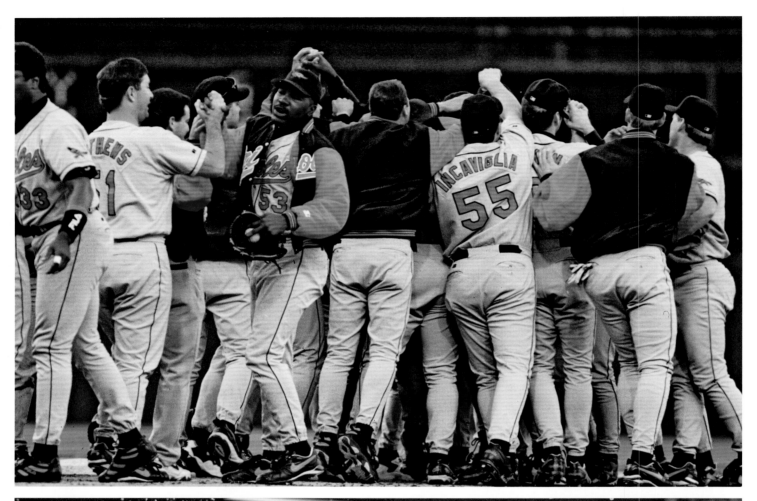

TOP: The Orioles celebrate their 1996 ALDS win over the Indians in Cleveland. It was their first postseason appearance in thirteen years.
ABOVE: Cal Ripken and Alan Mills see who can get the wettest as the Orioles celebrate their victory over the Mariners in the 1997 ALDS.

CAL RIPKEN JR.: THE IRON MAN

Cal Ripken Jr. will forever be tied to his amazing feat of having played 2,632 consecutive games, but his career cannot and should not be defined by the Streak—or the inevitable Iron Man tag he inherited from the legendary Lou Gehrig.

That feat alone is enough to set him apart from any other player in baseball history, and it rightly serves as Ripken's crowning achievement, but his story doesn't begin and end with the events of September 6, 1995, when he broke Gehrig's record of playing in 2,130 straight games. One has to examine his entire body of work in order to understand and appreciate the totality of the career—3,184 hits, 431 home runs, 3,001 games, two league Most Valuable Player Awards, two All-Star Game MVP citations, three postseason appearances, and one World Series championship.

Adding personal stuff to the equation, such as playing in his hometown, on the same team with his brother Bill and managed by his father, Cal Sr., adds another dimension. A lot of dreams were fulfilled and some were left incomplete, leaving an occasional mixed bag of emotions, but Ripken's baseball experience was truly a family affair.

"I was fortunate to have a long career, and the chance to play in my hometown for the team I grew up rooting for," Ripken said, looking back on his Hall of Fame career. "There were some challenges along the way—going through some 'down' times and seeing my dad lose his job, those were tough times for everybody."

Ripken's pro career started in 1982 with high expectations. "It started with a bang that first year. Knowing the history of the club, I kept wondering, 'When are we making our move?' after we started slowly," he recalled. "Then we got hot and went into the final weekend with a chance to win it, and that last series against Milwaukee was the most exciting I ever played in. We came up short in the last game, but I really think that series carried over to next year, when we won it all."

The 1983 season would provide Ripken with the highlight of his career. "The greatest feeling anybody could have is to catch the ball for the last out of the World Series," he said, recalling his reaction to catching a soft line drive off of what was Scott McGregor's last pitch of the Game 5 clincher against the Phillies. "At that point of my career, I thought we might experience that feeling a lot—but it didn't. I'm very grateful to have had that opportunity."

The years shortly after that World Series triumph were difficult ones. The club dabbled in free agency with mediocre results; Earl Weaver, who had retired after the 1982 season, made a comeback, replacing Joe Altobelli; but the club continued a downward trend, which led to trying times. "I was happy that dad got the job [in 1987] to manage the team, glad that he could fulfill that dream, but when he lost the job after six games the next year, it was hard to take. It was tough on me, tough on Bill, tough on Dad, and tough on the organization. I thought the problem was that we were in a rebuilding mode, but we never really admitted that we were rebuilding."

Frank Robinson replaced Cal Sr. as manager in the midst of what turned out to be a season-opening 21-game losing streak. "That period of time, with Dad losing his job and all the losing, was an extreme challenge," admitted Ripken. "It was a very dark period. Going 0-and-21, I wouldn't wish that on anybody. But, knowing now that I went through that, I'm glad I did because I don't know how anything could be tougher than that, and I feel like whatever challenge life throws, you can handle it."

As difficult as the 1987 and 1988 seasons were, the "Why Not?" year of 1989 rejuvenated Ripken. "When we took Toronto to the last series of year, it took me back to that Milwaukee series my first year," he said. "It was refreshing."

Ripken had his best year statistically, and his second MVP award, in 1991, when he felt "things just seemed to come together for me at the plate. I had gotten myself out of whack [the year before], Frank Robinson had helped me during that stretch, and things seemed to come together."

Through it all, as the Orioles gradually worked back into position for postseason play, and baseball suffered through two shortened seasons, causing a cancellation of the 1994 World Series and a delayed start in 1995, Ripken's pursuit of Gehrig's record became a national story that played out almost daily. There were times when he felt compelled to defend himself for playing every day.

"It was the way I was brought up," he said. "Dad's philosophy was come to the park ready to play every day; you can't do anything about yesterday, and you can't play tomorrow's game ahead of time; just be ready to play every day."

Rather than look at the streak in its entirety, Ripken always felt it was a culmination of many mini-streaks. "I always looked at it as a combination of 162-game streaks, not the overall number," he said. "It's not like you played all those games without ever having time off."

The Streak is not a subject he's inclined to dwell on, but there are aspects of his longevity that are appealing to Ripken. "One of the coolest things about the Streak for me," he said, "is how it is related to reliability—that you're someone who can be counted on. I like it when I hear stories of people being compared to the Streak for not missing a day of work or a day of school. That's not something I ever did—I didn't have perfect attendance in school."

Ripken and the Orioles got back to the postseason in 1996 and 1997, but Ripken never duplicated that feeling of catching the ball for the final out of the 1983 World Series. He did, however, get a fitting personal farewell thrill in his final season in 2001; during the All-Star Game, he hit a home run that led to his second All-Star MVP Award.

"Personally, I really wanted to play [the All-Star Game] one more time, and fortunately I was able to do that," Ripken admitted. "I wanted to go back and be a teammate with the best players in the league one more time. It was very special. When I hit the home run, it was a magical feeling."

Not a bad way to finish—closing out a Hall of Fame career on the All-Star stage.

MEMORABLE GAMES
1992–1997

April 6, 1992

Oriole Park at Camden Yards opens to rave reviews, changing the face of baseball parks forever. Rick Sutcliffe tosses a five-hit shutout as the Orioles down the Cleveland Indians, 2–0, in a nifty two hours and two minutes. Chris Hoiles doubles home one run, and Bill Ripken squeezes home the other run in front of 44,568 fans.

September 6, 1995

Cal Ripken becomes baseball's "Iron Man" playing in his 2,131st consecutive game to break Lou Gehrig's record. Ripken goes 2-for-4 and homers for the second night in a row as the Orioles beat the Angels, 4–2. When the game becomes official in the middle of the fifth inning, a celebration ensues, and teammates Bobby Bonilla and Rafael Palmeiro push Ripken out of the dugout to take his now-famous lap around the ballpark, starting precisely at 9:31 p.m., or 21:31 in military time.

June 6, 1993

In the seventh inning of a game at Camden Yards, Seattle catcher Bill Haselman charges the mound after getting hit by a Mike Mussina pitch. In the ensuing melee, Cal Ripken strains his right knee, saying later it was the closest he ever came to ending his consecutive games streak. It was game 1,790 of the streak. Eight players eventually are suspended. The Orioles win, 5–2.

May 17, 1996

Chris Hoiles's grand slam with two outs and a full count lifts the Orioles to a 14–13 win over Seattle at Camden Yards, only the fourth time in history a game has been won by one run on a two-out, sudden-death grand slam. Rafael Palmeiro drives in six runs as the Orioles out-hit the Mariners, 21–20.

September 6, 1996

Eddie Murray hits his 500th career homer off Detroit's Felipe Lira. The seventh-inning solo blast comes minutes before midnight in a rain-delayed game on the one-year anniversary of Cal Ripken's record-breaking consecutive game. Unfortunately, the Orioles lose to the Tigers, 5–4, in 12 innings.

October 5, 1996

Roberto Alomar ties the game with a two-out, ninth-inning single, and his 12th-inning homer gives the Orioles a 4–3 win as the Orioles beat the Indians, 3-games-to-1, in the AL Division Series. Randy Myers retires the side in the 12th for the Orioles, whose 88–74 record earned them the AL wild card berth.

May 30, 1997

Mike Mussina retires the first 25 Cleveland batters before Sandy Alomar lines a 2–0 pitch to left for a single with one out in the ninth inning, ending the right-hander's perfect game bid. Mussina strikes out the final two batters for his second one-hit victory, 3–0. It was the tenth time an Oriole pitcher had a no-hitter broken up in the ninth inning, the last until Daniel Cabrera on September 28, 2006, at New York.

October 15, 1997

Cleveland's Tony Fernandez breaks up a scoreless game with an 11th-inning homer off Armando Benitez, giving the Indians a 1–0 win over the O's to take the ALCS, 4-games-to-2. Mike Mussina allows one hit over eight innings in that game, and he goes winless in two starts in the series, despite allowing one run over 15 innings with 29 strikeouts.

October 9, 1996

In the eighth inning of ALCS Game 1 at Yankee Stadium, twelve-year-old Jeffrey Maier reaches over the right field wall and interferes with Tony Tarasco's attempted catch of Derek Jeter's fly ball, but umpire Richie Garcia rules it a game-tying homer. Bernie Williams homers in the 12th inning to win the game, 5–4, and the Yankees go on to win the series in five games.

October 5, 1997

In the Division Series, Manager Davey Johnson starts Jerome Walton at first base and Jeff Reboulet at second in place of regulars Rafael Palmeiro and Roberto Alomar in Games 1 and 4 against Mariners lefty Randy Johnson, and the move pays off. The Orioles win the first game, 9–3, and Reboulet's first-inning homer off Johnson in Game 4 at Camden Yards propels the Birds to a 3–1 win and the series victory.

August 12, 1997

One night after longtime public address announcer Rex Barney passes away, the Orioles pay tribute in their game against the A's by leaving his seat in the press box empty and using no PA or music from the sound system. Scott Erickson tosses a three-hit shutout as the O's win, 8–0, before 46,925 fans at Camden Yards. Rex's seat remains empty the remainder of the season; guest PA announcers use a space in the video production room.

CHAPTER 13

MAKEOVER MODE

Ultimately, the era following the back-to-back postseason runs of 1996 and 1997 would come to be known as "the drought." Despite successive postseason appearances, including 1997's wire-to-wire run to a division title, the Orioles were showing their age, much like what happened to the 1983 World Series team.

That may or may not have influenced Davey Johnson, who said he wouldn't manage a third season without an extension. Johnson resigned in November 1997, and the club turned over the manager's job to pitching coach Ray Miller. At the outset, it looked like the O's might not miss a beat. They came out of the gate with 10 wins in the first 12 games, but those dozen games did little beyond raise false hopes.

The Orioles went 69–81 the rest of the way, stumbling home with a 79–83 record and finishing in fourth place in 1998, a position that would become all too familiar over the next decade. Probably the most significant development of Miller's first year at the helm came on September 20, when Ryan Minor started at third base in place of Cal Ripken, who voluntarily ended his major league–record consecutive-games streak at 2,632 in the Orioles final home game of the season.

Before the 1999 season began, the Orioles made two major announcements. Having had a degree of success with free agents while putting together the '96 and '97 teams, the Orioles signed veteran outfielder Albert Belle to a five-year contract that gave the team the highest payroll in baseball. Belle's numbers for two years justified the contract—he batted .289 with 60 homers and 220 RBIs between 1999 and 2000—but a lingering hip injury sidelined him permanently in the spring of 2001, and he never played another game.

Then, Orioles owner Peter Angelos arranged for the Orioles to play an historic two-game series against a team of Cuban all-stars; the hope was that the exhibition games would promote closer cultural and social ties between the two

OPPOSITE: Melvin Mora, a utility player who was one of four players acquired from the Mets for shortstop Mike Bordick in July 2000, shuttled between shortstop, center field, and left field for three seasons with the Orioles before taking over at third base in 2004. By the time he left after the 2009 season, Mora had played more games at third for the Orioles than anyone but Brooks Robinson. A two-time All-Star, he set the club record with a .340 batting average in 2004 and led the league with a .419 on-base percentage. Overall, he batted .280 with 158 home runs in 10 seasons with the Orioles.

LEFT: Drafted by basketball's Philadelphia 76ers in the second round and by the Orioles in the 33rd round in 1996 after a two-sport career at the University of Oklahoma, Ryan Minor spent parts of four seasons in the majors, three with the Orioles. In his third big league game, he started at third base on September 20, 1998, when Cal Ripken Jr. ended his consecutive game streak at 2,632.

ABOVE: Shortstop Miguel Tejada signed a six-year free agent contract with the Orioles and in his first season, 2004, batted .311 with 34 home runs and a then–club record 150 RBIs, helping the team finish third in the AL East after six straight fourth-place finishes. But the team fell to fourth during the next three seasons, and Tejada was traded to Houston for five players. He returned to play third base in 2010 and finished his five seasons as an Oriole with a .305 batting average, 109 homers, and 468 RBIs.

OPPOSITE TOP: The centerpiece of a five-for-one trade with the Mariners in February 2008, Adam Jones grew into an All-Star and Gold Glove–winning center fielder with the Orioles. He signed a six-year contract extension in May 2012.

OPPOSITE BOTTOM: Claimed on waivers from the Indians before the 2007 season, Jeremy Guthrie started the year in the bullpen before moving into the starting rotation mid-year and led the Orioles in innings pitched over his final four seasons with the team, averaging 192 innings over his five years. He led the team in wins three times but also led the American League with 17 losses in 2009 and 2011.

nations that transcended baseball. In late March, the Orioles ventured to Havana, the first time an American professional team had played in Cuba in forty years, and the Cuban team played at Camden Yards in May.

The Cuba series turned out to be one of the few highlights of the season. When the Orioles finished the 1999 season with an almost identical record (78–84) as the year before and another fourth-place finish, Miller became the first of seven managers who would come and go during the longest seasonal losing streak in club history.

By 2000, the "drought" was in full swing. Mike Mussina left via free agency that year, Mike Hargrove moved into the manager's office, and Syd Thrift was the general manager. The Orioles were in full "makeover" mode and traded veterans that returned 17 players, mostly prospects expected to move to the big-league roster in the years to come. Most never saw Baltimore, and only one of the acquired players had any lasting impact. Melvin Mora was regarded as a part-time utility player when he arrived in a package deal with the Mets in July 2000. Eventually, Mora landed at third base for the last six of his nine-and-a-half seasons with the Orioles, playing more games at third than anyone except Brooks Robinson, and in 2004 Mora set the club's single-season batting mark with a .340 average.

In the early years of the "drought," most of the good news about the Orioles revolved around Ripken: first, the ending of his consecutive-games streak, then

" Angelos lured the son of former O's general manager Lee MacPhail back to his birthplace and handed him the task of reshaping the organization."

his 400th home run, his 3,000th hit, and his second All-Star Game MVP Award in 2001—two and a half months before his retirement. Even during those difficult times, no one thought that, by the time Ripken was elected to the Hall of Fame in 2007, the Orioles would still be looking for a winning season.

The other good news entailed Orioles fans. In 2007, the club launched OriolesREACH, strengthening and broadening its role in giving back to the community with a variety of programs and initiatives to assist charities, organizations, and individuals, both at the ballpark and throughout the region. Today, more than 50,000 youth annually are treated to games at Oriole Park at Camden Yards through programs sponsored by the club and its players, and upwards of $3 million annually is contributed to organizations in cash and in-kind contributions. In 2008, the Orioles also welcomed the 50 millionth fan to Oriole Park at Camden Yards, reaching that milestone faster than any other sports facility in American history.

Not long after Ripken's 2007 Hall of Fame induction, the Orioles made a key move in the front office, bringing Andy MacPhail in to oversee baseball operations. Owner Peter Angelos had been impressed with MacPhail, having worked with him on various ownership committees. Ultimately, Angelos lured the son of former O's general manager Lee MacPhail back to his birthplace and handed him the task of reshaping the organization.

Before MacPhail's arrival, the Orioles had a brief run under Lee Mazzilli, who succeeded Hargrove as manager. In 2005, the Orioles went 42–28 before losing

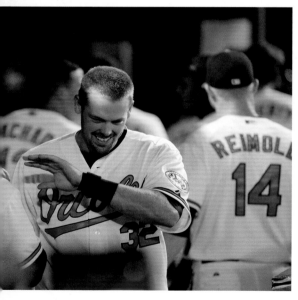

TOP: Two-time All-Star Brian Roberts spent six full seasons and parts of six others as the Orioles' second baseman, from 2001 to 2013. His 56 doubles in 2009 were the most ever by an Oriole and most by a switch-hitter in MLB history. A concussion and other injuries limited him to 195 games over his final four seasons with the Orioles.

ABOVE: Matt Wieters was the Orioles first-round pick in the 2007 draft and became the team's starting catcher when he was called up midway through the 2009 season.

60 of the last 92 games, a streak that cost Mazzilli his job, and put Sam Perlozzo in the manager's office. Dave Trembley replaced Perlozzo as manager during the 2007 season, but the club still did not have the pieces in place to improve markedly. After spending the last two months of 2007 evaluating the team, MacPhail came to a simple conclusion and made moves that would improve the club in lasting ways. "I felt the only way to improve the team," he said later, "was to trade the two best players—[shortstop Miguel] Tejada and [pitcher Erik] Bedard."

The only thing better than that decision was the result. Tejada was the first to go, on December 12, 2007, when he was dealt to Houston for pitchers Troy Patton, Matt Albers, and Dennis Sarfate, outfielder Luke Scott, and infielder Michael Costanzo. It took MacPhail another two months to pull off what proved to be his biggest heist. Just before spring training opened, on February 8, 2008, Bedard went to Seattle in exchange for outfielder Adam Jones, and pitchers Chris Tillman, Tony Butler, George Sherrill, and Kam Mickolio.

In a span of two months, the Orioles traded two players for 10, including seven pitchers under the age of twenty-seven. It was the beginning of MacPhail's "grow the arms, buy the bats" philosophy. Though the plan took a while to get off the ground, it helped the team make positive strides. The Orioles got direct and indirect results from both trades, both on the field in Baltimore and in follow-up trades involving Sherrill and Mickolio. A couple of other trades and acquisitions brought J. J. Hardy, Chris Davis, and Tommy Hunter to the Orioles, and these players would ultimately become core performers as the O's finally turned the corner.

As good as those trades were, they were only part of MacPhail's legacy. On July 29, 2010, MacPhail chose Buck Showalter to succeed interim skipper Juan Samuel, who had replaced Trembley as the Orioles manager. This move, just a few days before Showalter's minor league manager and mentor Johnny Oates was inducted into the club's Hall of Fame, brought much-needed stability, even if it wasn't the final piece of the puzzle.

For the rest of the 2010 season, the Orioles showed signs of immediate improvement, going 34–23 the rest of the way. But there was still a lot of work to do. In 2011, despite the advantage of having his first spring training camp with his new team, Showalter got a quick glimpse of what the six managers who preceded him had dealt with over the previous eleven years. In the end, the Orioles 69–93 record for 2011 was only a modest three-game improvement over a near-disastrous 2010.

One area of clear improvement was the major league team's new spring training facility in Sarasota, Florida, which opened at the start the 2010 season. This enabled the Orioles to merge their major league and minor league operations in the same city for the first time in two decades. Ed Smith Stadium, where the major league team trained, was completely renovated in 2011, giving the team a fan-friendly training facility with all of the modern amenities needed for players and fans alike. Today, the facilities at Ed Smith Stadium and at the Buck O'Neil Baseball Complex at Twin Lakes Park, where the club's minor leaguers work out, not only host Orioles spring training but also serve as a year-round host for professional and amateur baseball activities, as well as family-friendly and community events.

Andy MacPhail stepped down as general manager after 2011, but at the end of the season he experienced a taste of something the Orioles hadn't done in a long time—finish strong by winning a few significant games in September, a development about which the Red Sox would attest.

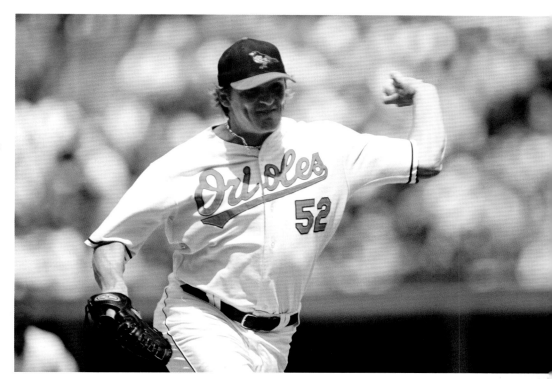

TOP: Acquired from the Reds in July 1999, B. J. Ryan went from left-handed relief specialist to late-inning set-up man before supplanting Jorge Julio as the Orioles' closer in the final weeks of the 2004 season. In 2005 he saved 36 games, then signed a five-year, $47 million contract with the Blue Jays and had two effective seasons with Toronto before arm injuries ended his career.

BOTTOM: A third-generation big leaguer, Jerry Hairston reached the majors in his second pro season after being drafted in 1997. In 2001 he established himself at second base and led the club in stolen bases for two seasons, but after an injury early in the 2003 season, he lost the starting job to Brian Roberts. Moving to the outfield in 2004, he missed half the season with trips to the disabled list and was traded after the season to the Cubs for Sammy Sosa.

 At the end of the season he experienced a taste of something the Orioles hadn't done in a long time—finish strong by winning a few significant games in September, a development about which the Red Sox would attest."

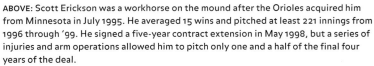

ABOVE: Scott Erickson was a workhorse on the mound after the Orioles acquired him from Minnesota in July 1995. He averaged 15 wins and pitched at least 221 innings from 1996 through '99. He signed a five-year contract extension in May 1998, but a series of injuries and arm operations allowed him to pitch only one and a half of the final four years of the deal.

ABOVE RIGHT: Although known as "Mr. Marlin," Jeff Conine spent six years with the Orioles, playing first, third, and the outfield in two stretches with the club (1999–2003 and 2006). He was voted Most Valuable Oriole in 2001 when he led the club with a .311 average and 97 RBIs.

RIGHT: A Rule 5 pick from Toronto, Jay Gibbons led AL rookies with 15 homers before breaking his hand in August 2001. He hit a career-high 28 homers the next season and was Most Valuable Oriole in 2003, batting .277 with 23 homers and 100 RBIs. He hit 121 homers in seven seasons with the Orioles.

OPPOSITE TOP: Despite carrying a losing record in seven of his eight seasons with the Orioles, Sidney Ponson was a mainstay of the starting rotation from 1998 through 2005. In 2003 he was among the AL's top pitchers with a 14–6 record and 3.77 ERA through July when he was traded to the Giants, but his 14 wins led the club for the season. He re-signed with the Orioles after the season as a free agent and pitched two more seasons in Baltimore, finishing with a 73–85 record and 4.86 ERA in his Orioles career but ranking among the club leaders in losses, starts, and innings pitched.

OPPOSITE FAR RIGHT: Left-hander Erik Bedard spent six seasons with the Orioles (2002–07), led the club in wins in 2006 and 2007, and set the team's single-season strikeout mark with 221 in 2007. After that season, he was traded to Seattle for five players, including promising center fielder Adam Jones and right-handed pitcher Chris Tillman.

OPPOSITE LEFT: From 2002 through 2006, Rodrigo Lopez was the Orioles' most dependable starter, winning 60 games and getting the opening day nod three times. He won 15 games twice but led the AL with 18 losses in 2006.

MEMORABLE GAMES
1998–2010

August 21, 1998

Cal Ripken gets his 2,849th hit, a seventh-inning single, to pass Brooks Robinson as the O's all-time hits leader, in a 6–3 loss to the Indians at Camden Yards.

June 13, 1999

Cal Ripken sets club records, going six-for-six and scoring five runs, as the Orioles pound Atlanta, 22–1, at Turner Field. Ripken has a double and two home runs and drives in six runs. Will Clark's four hits and five RBIs are overlooked in the O's 25-hit attack as Ripken becomes the only Oriole to get six hits or score five runs in a game.

April 15, 2000

Playing in his 2,800th major league game, Cal Ripken gets his 3,000th career hit, a single off Hector Carrasco at Minnesota. Ripken becomes the 24th player to reach 3,000 hits and only the seventh to get 3,000 hits and 400 home runs in major league history.

September 20, 1998

Just prior to the last home game of the season, Cal Ripken voluntarily asks Manager Ray Miller to take him out of the lineup, ending Ripken's consecutive-games streak at 2,632 games. Ryan Minor starts at third base, and the Orioles lose to the Yankees, 5–4.

August 17, 1999

Jesse Orosco enters the game in the seventh inning at Camden Yards and retires Minnesota's Todd Walker on a fly out for the final out to set a major league record with his 1,072nd career pitching appearance, passing Dennis Eckersley. Ultimately, Orosco appears in 1,252 games in his twenty-four-year career.

April 1, 2002

Tony Batista hits a grand slam and the Orioles score eight runs off Roger Clemens, spoiling his debut with the Yankees in a 10–3 win on Opening Day at Camden Yards. Later that evening, the University of Maryland's men's basketball team wins the NCAA title, capping a memorable day in Charm City.

September 29, 2004

In the first game of a doubleheader sweep of Toronto, Miguel Tejada singles to drive in his 143rd run, breaking the club's single-season record. Three days later, his 212th hit sets the Orioles' single-season record. He finishes the first year of a six-year contract with 214 hits and 153 RBIs.

October 6, 2001

Having announced in May his plans to retire at season's end, Cal Ripken plays his last game in front of 48,807 fans at Camden Yards. The Orioles' last game of the season originally was scheduled to be played at Yankees Stadium, but the events of 9/11 force changes to the MLB schedule that allow Ripken to end his career at home.

June 30, 2009

The Orioles overcome a 10-1 deficit with five runs in the bottom of the 7th inning and five more in the 8th to beat Boston 11-10, the club's biggest comeback win ever.

March 31, 2003

In the season opener at Camden Yards, the Indians score two runs when Ellis Burks's fly ball gets lost amid the falling snow. Marty Cordova's two-run homer ties the game in the eighth inning for the Orioles. The Birds retie the game in the 12th inning on an Indians passed ball with two outs, then win 6–5 in the 13th inning on Gary Matthews's single.

CHAPTER 14

A SEASON— AND MORE— TO REMEMBER

Robert Andino isn't to be found anywhere in the team's record book, but he's a household name among those who treasure Orioles' lore, thanks to the role he played in the stunning comeback win that many believe signaled the end of "the drought."

The longest continuous losing streak in club history, fourteen years, wasn't officially put to rest until September 2012, when the Orioles finally clinched their first winning season since the wire-to-wire season of 1997. But the final game of 2011 set the stage for the Orioles breakthrough the next year. As had been the case in each of the preceding thirteen seasons, the Orioles were winding up a dreadful year, having lost more than 90 games for the sixth straight time. No one expected that September 29, 2011, would become a date to remember.

For the Orioles' opponent, the Red Sox, the game meant a great deal. They needed a win to assure at least a tie for a postseason spot. The Red Sox took a 3–2 lead into the ninth inning, which opened with ace reliever Jonathan Papelbon striking out Adam Jones and Mark Reynolds. That's when the long-dormant "Orioles Magic" made an unexpected return.

Chris Davis ripped a double into the right-field corner, and those in the Camden Yards crowd of 29,749 who were heading for the exits hesitated. Then, almost before Joe Angel in the radio booth or Gary Thorne on the TV side could say, "Tying run in scoring position," Nolan Reimold slammed a drive to right-center field, a one-hopper over the fence, tying the game. Suddenly, the winning run was at second base.

Now it was up to Robert Andino, an unlikely hero perhaps but in the perfect spot for the biggest hit of his career—a line drive single to left that drove in the winning run. As the Orioles erupted in wild celebration, the Red Sox stood in stunned disbelief.

OPPOSITE: After four years spent mainly as a set-up man in the bullpen, Jim Johnson led the American League with 51 saves in 2012 and 50 saves in 2013, becoming only the third reliever in history to record 50 or more saves twice. Traded to the A's after the 2013 season, he ranks second on the Orioles' all-time saves list with 122.

FOLLOWING PAGES: Nate McLouth swings at a pitch during a game against the Indians in June 2013, the second of his two seasons as an outfielder with the Orioles.

Despite their uninspiring 69–93 record, the Orioles closed the 2011 season with 11 wins in their last 16 games, all against contending teams, including five of their last seven against the Red Sox. The come-from-behind, one-run victory in that final game would become a staple of success the following year—and it may very well have been made possible by a perfectly executed relay from Adam Jones in center field to shortstop J. J. Hardy to catcher Matt Wieters, 8-6-2 in the score-card, which prevented the Red Sox from scoring a potential insurance run in the eighth inning.

After the wild finish to the 2011 season, the Orioles celebrated in postseason style, and manager Buck Showalter noted the obvious difference in emotions. "That's the only time I haven't talked to a team after the final game of the season," he admitted. "It's pretty tough to top that. Not much to say."

The manager also appreciated what the Red Sox were feeling, as their post-season berth slipped away in the time it took to throw a half-dozen pitches. "I can't believe what Boston must be going through. . . . We understand that there is another side to this. Baseball is a cruel game," said Showalter. On the one hand, one win helped alleviate the agony of 93 losses, while one loss could also negate an entire season.

And both, it turned out, had a lasting carryover effect.

The electrifying win in the last game of the O's 2011 season provided hope for the immediate future. Indeed, Dan Duquette, who was named vice president for baseball operations in November 2011, emphasized that attitude and focus were needed more than hope. At his introductory press conference, he said that Earl Weaver's book, *Weaver on Strategy*, would become required reading throughout the player development system, harkening a return to the old "Oriole Way." The results were immediate.

Fast forward to May 6, 2012: Andino hit a three-run home run, Hardy hit a cou-ple of solo shots, and in the 16th inning the potential winning run was thrown out at the plate—Jones to Hardy to Wieters, 8-6-2 once again, as the Orioles beat the Red Sox, 9–6, in a game that went 17 innings. Later, this early spring game came to sym-bolize a turnaround season to remember, one in which the team continually found ways to defy the odds and rekindle memories of the Orioles' glory years.

After enduring sub-.500 baseball for 14 consecutive years, the tone for this turnaround season was set early with a three-game opening series sweep of the Twins. Despite losing the next three to the Yankees, including the only two regular season extra-inning games they would lose all year, the Orioles went the rest of the way without one day below the break-even mark. Early in that run, on May

OPPOSITE: Infielder Robert Andino celebrates after beating Texas in the first-ever AL Wild Card playoff game in 2012, marking the Orioles' first postseason appearance in fifteen years.
ABOVE: Another walk-off win! Chris Davis lifts Nate McLouth, whose RBI single in the ninth beat Tampa Bay on September 12, 2012.

1, Buck Showalter recorded his 1,000th win as a major league manager, a 7–1 win over the Yankees, his first team, after which he was playfully doused by his energetic troops.

Five days later, the May 6 win became one of 16 straight extra-inning wins, the longest such streak in the major leagues since the Cleveland Indians won 17 in a row in 1949. The Orioles, who had only a 712–705 edge in runs for the season, outscored their opponents 33–5 in a total of 60 extra innings. In addition, they gave a whole new meaning to the term "close to the edge," going 54–23 in games decided by two or fewer runs, and 29–9 in those decided by one, including a remarkable 13 one-run wins in a row between June 22 and September 1.

Throughout most of the season, the Orioles operated at a significant run differential, which the experts freely predicted would be their undoing. Shortly after the All-Star break, on July 17, the Orioles' record dropped to 46–44, and they were 10 games behind the first-place Yankees and seemingly on the verge of dropping out of contention.

But as Showalter pointed out often during the course of the year, the Orioles "set the bar high for themselves, and didn't look back." Starting with the 91st game, things began to change, slowly at first, and by the time heralded rookie infielder Manny Machado arrived on August 9, the thought of another "Why Not?" season was on the minds of many. In a late-August session with the media, Showalter professed not to like amusement park roller coasters. "We got one-run games—I get on a roller coaster every night, and they don't put a bar down," he said. With the Orioles still in the hunt, "BUCKle Up" became the catch phrase of the season's final month.

By September 11, the Orioles and Yankees were tied for the lead in the American League East with 79–62 records, and the last three weeks were like a close finish in a marathon. The Orioles never got the lead, but they never trailed by more than one and a half games. As late as September 29, they tied the Yankees again, with three games to play. Then, while stranded in the airport in Jacksonville, Florida, after an emergency layover en route to their last three games in Tampa Bay, the team learned that they had clinched a wild-card playoff spot. The Orioles exchanged high-fives as their flight resumed to Tampa, still intent on overtaking the Yankees. When two losses against Tampa Bay eliminated the Orioles from first-place contention, they had to go to Texas for the first-ever "play-in" wild-card game against the Rangers. In a new playoff wrinkle, Major League Baseball had created a second wild-card spot in 2012, and the winner of a one-game playoff between wild-card teams would move on to the Division Series.

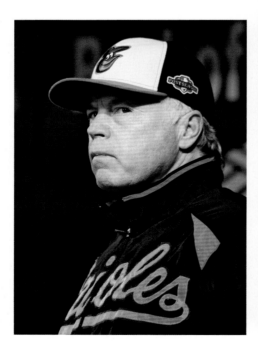

RIGHT: Buck Showalter became the Orioles' 19th manager on July 29, 2010, reminding many fans of legendary skipper Earl Weaver. Showalter guided the Orioles into the postseason in two of his first four full seasons as manager.
FAR RIGHT: J. J. Hardy has continued the Orioles' tradition of excellent shortstops, joining the club in 2011 and earning two Gold Gloves and an All-Star berth while batting .259 with 86 homers in his first four seasons. He signed a three-year contract extension on the eve of the 2014 postseason.

The odds were seemingly stacked against the Orioles. The Rangers had won five of seven regular-season games between the teams, three of them by seven or more runs, outscoring the Orioles 56–24 in the process. In addition, the O's starting pitcher for the wild-card playoff, Joe Saunders, who was obtained in a trade with Arizona only six weeks before, had never won a game in Texas during the six years he pitched for the Angels, going 0–6 with a 9.38 ERA.

The Orioles diverted from their normal script; they avoided their typical one-run or extra-inning nail-biter. Instead, with the scored tied 1–1 through five innings, they pushed across a run in the top of the sixth. Saunders finished the bottom of the sixth inning, then turned the game over to the bullpen. Darren O'Day pitched two scoreless innings, Brian Matusz got a key eighth-inning strikeout, and the Orioles scratched out three more runs over the last three innings. Then, in the bottom of the ninth, Jim Johnson survived a bases-loaded, two-out situation to seal the 5–1 win and a spot in the American League Division Series against the Yankees.

"We talked about it being 'sudden life,' not 'sudden death,'" said Showalter, "and that's the way we played. It's a real proud moment for us. This is for our fans."

In fact, Orioles fans took to the streets in a celebration reminiscent of the team's three World Series wins. Some two thousand miles away, the players did the same, finally able to enjoy the fruits of a long, unpredictable season and relishing the thought of a postseason game at home. "It's going to be an incredible atmosphere," said Johnson, which turned out to be an understatement.

Even though he'd only been with the team a few weeks, Joe Saunders enjoyed the moment perhaps even more than his new teammates. Growing up in northern Virginia, he was an Orioles' fan at a young age. "Having watched this team since I was a kid and now being a part of this, watching these guys celebrate, it's a special feeling," he said.

The first two ALDS games were held at Camden Yards, and not even a two-hour-and-forty-one-minute rain delay before the first game could dampen the enthusiastic atmosphere. By the ninth inning, the score was tied 2–2, and the O's crowd anticipated another close victory, but the Yankees scored five times in the ninth inning for a 7–2 win. The Orioles rebounded for a 3–2 win in Game 2, winning the type of tight contest they had all year. Then they went to New York with the series even and high hopes for extending the season.

TOP: The first Taiwanese-born player in Orioles history, Wei-Yin Chen won 35 games in his first three seasons with the Orioles, twice leading the team in wins, including a 16–6 mark with a 3.54 ERA in 2014.

ABOVE: Nick Markakis manned right field for nine seasons with the Orioles (2006–14), winning two Gold Gloves and batting .290 with 141 homers. His 1,547 hits and 316 doubles rank sixth in club history.

LEFT: Nate McLouth congratulates Manny Machado after the second of his home runs on August 10, 2012, helped beat the Royals 7–1. Machado became the first player to record a triple and two homers in his first two big league games.

OPPOSITE: Acquired from Texas in 2011, Chris Davis not only played an excellent first base for the Orioles but filled in at third base and right field and, in a 17-inning game at Boston on May 6, 2012, pitched the final two innings to become the first position player to record a win for the Orioles.

FOLLOWING PAGES: The view from the right-field upper deck—Manny Machado has just homered against Seattle on August 3, 2013.

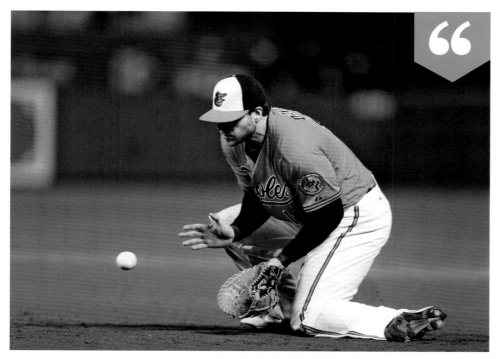

Watching how they played the game every day, the standard they held themselves to, and the way they set the bar high in Baltimore . . . it's been about as much fun as I have ever had in the big leagues."

But the Orioles' extra-inning magic ran out in Game 3: the Yankees' Raul Ibanez hit a game-tying pinch-hit home run in the ninth and a game-winner in the 11th. Remarkably, the Orioles bounced back in Game 4: with the score tied 1–1 in the 13th inning, J. J. Hardy doubled to drive in the winning run, a 2–1 O's victory that evened the series again. In Game 5, Yankees' starter C. C. Sabathia held the ace card, restricting the Orioles to a lone run in a 3–1 win that, finally, brought the season of the "BUCKle Up Birds" to a disappointing, yet fulfilling close.

In a way, the series with the Yankees was a mirror image of the 2012 season for the Orioles, and it brought a touch of irony. Four of the five games were decided by one or two runs—each team winning a pair. Two games went extra innings, with the teams again splitting the decisions. All told on the season, the Orioles played 20 extra-inning games, winning 17, with all three losses coming at the hands of the Yankees—the first two in the first week of the season, and the final one in the playoffs.

"Watching how they played the game every day, the standard they held themselves to, and the way they set the bar high in Baltimore . . . it's been about as much fun as I have ever had in the big leagues," Showalter said, summing up a year that finally put the longest losing stretch to rest and set the stage for the start of something new, yet reminiscent of something old—the "Glory Years" of seasons past.

The magic didn't completely carry over into the 2013 season, but with several young stars emerging, the Orioles did validate their emergence as a force to be reckoned with in the American League's Eastern Division. Chris Davis led the majors with a club-record 53 home runs. Chris Tillman won 18 games, and three Orioles—centerfielder Adam Jones, shortstop J. J. Hardy, and third baseman Manny Machado in his first full season—won Gold Gloves. The Orioles stayed competitive all year, remaining in contention until the final weeks of the season and finishing with an 85–77 record, a strong indication that 2012 was not a fluke but a sign of new times.

If the 2013 season produced a "hangover" effect because of expectations from the year before, it also left a feeling of unfinished business and even a degree of urgency as the Orioles gathered in Sarasota, Florida, to prepare for 2014, their 60th anniversary season.

Their appetite had been whetted by a slice of the postseason pie in 2012, and they had validated their status as a legitimate contender by following up the breakthrough year with 85 wins. While some hinted about a small window of

opportunity, Duquette and Manager Showalter saw a team with a solid core of young players in need of only minor tweaking in order to establish itself as a key player in the American League's powerful Eastern Division. Showalter had a nucleus of players who fit his "want to" description, and it remained for Duquette to deliver a few more "can do" performers to supplement a roster that would continually evolve as the season progressed.

It took awhile for some of the pieces to fall into place, but the Orioles didn't waver in their commitment to add a pitcher for the starting rotation and a power hitter to bolster a lineup that led the American League with 212 home runs in 2013. Just when it appeared spring training would open without an additional veteran presence, Duquette pulled the trigger on two major free-agent signings.

On February 19, in time to join the pitchers and catchers in camp, right-hander Ubaldo Jimenez agreed to a four-year contract—and five days later, just as the position players were reporting, Nelson Cruz agreed to a one-year contract, giving Showalter an additional right-handed power bat for the middle of the lineup.

Even though Jimenez would struggle his first year in Baltimore, he brought a veteran presence to the rotation, and his addition, along with that of Cruz, served notice that the Orioles would be a factor in the highly competitive AL East. However, few could have predicted the path they would ultimately follow.

There had been one key move made early in the off-season that, though generally understated at the time, proved to be pivotal. On October 29, the Orioles hired Dave Wallace as their new pitching coach, and at his suggestion they brought in Dom Chiti as the bullpen coach. As spring turned into summer, it became obvious that the long-awaited turnaround of a young pitching staff was in progress.

Widely respect throughout baseball, Wallace brought his unique "How can we help you?" approach to a pitching staff that had previously been in constant flux. He and Chiti, a former minor league pitcher and coach in the O's system, had previously worked together in the Atlanta organization, and they brought a relaxed style that quickly resonated with their young pupils.

Though they had a basically set roster, the Orioles still had some issues to deal with in preparation for the opening of the season. Third baseman Manny Machado finished 2013 on the disabled list, the result of a knee injury that required surgery and would keep him out of the lineup for the first month of 2014. It would prove to be only the first of several physical issues encountered by the club during the season.

The Orioles opened with a 2–1 win over the Red Sox, but a four-game losing streak at the hands of the Red Sox and Tigers quickly followed, producing the first "crucial" game of the year on April 6, a crisis Chris Tillman handled with a 3–1 win over the Tigers.

The first month was not without further incident. Chris Davis, who in 2013 led the major league with 53 home runs but was struggling through the early weeks of the 2014 season, suffered an oblique injury on April 24 and went on the

OPPOSITE TOP: After being the fourth overall pick in the 2012 draft, right-hander Kevin Gausman got his first taste of the majors in 2013 and established himself in the rotation in June 2014, going 7–7 with a 3.57 ERA in 20 starts. He allowed one run in eight innings in relief in the 2014 postseason.

OPPOSITE BOTTOM: After hitting 33 homers in his first full season with the Orioles in 2012, Chris Davis exploded in 2013, setting a club record and leading the majors with 53 home runs.

BELOW: After splitting time between the minors and the starting rotation for three seasons, lefty Zach Britton established himself as the Orioles closer in 2014, with 37 saves in 41 chances and a 1.65 ERA.

RIGHT: Manager Buck Showalter and Executive Vice President for Baseball Operations Dan Duquette have guided the Orioles to two postseason appearances in their first three seasons together, including the 2014 AL East Division title. Showalter has gone 377–328 since taking over as manager in July 2010. The Orioles have finished over .500 in each of the three seasons since Duquette joined the club in November 2011, for the first time since 1997.

BELOW: Nelson Cruz, signed to a one-year contract in 2014, batted .271 with 108 RBIs and led the majors with 40 home runs to help the Orioles to the AL East title. Coming behind Chris Davis' 53 homers in 2013, it was the first time two different players from the same team led the majors in home runs in back-to-back seasons since the Yankees' Lou Gehrig and Joe DiMaggio did it in 1936–37.

disabled list two days later. While nothing good ever comes from an injury, the Orioles caught a major break with the timing.

Steve Pearce, who had been with four organizations the year before, including two stints each with the Orioles and Yankees, had been designated for assignment on April 22 to make room for pitcher T. J. McFarland. Because he was replacing an injured player and had rejected a waiver claim by the Blue Jays, Pearce was able to rejoin the Orioles on May 1, a transaction that would prove to be the most vital of his career. That date also marked the return of Machado to the lineup, a move that figured to solidify the Orioles' lineup and allow Ryan Flaherty and rookie Jonathan Schoop to concentrate solely on second base.

With Cruz off to a powerful start, Adam Jones maintaining the pace he'd established the previous two years (averaging over 30 HRs and hitting over .285), and Gold Glove catcher Matt Wieters off to the best offensive start of his career, the Orioles appeared poised to glide on cruise control the rest of the way. That thought proved temporary, however. By the time Davis came off the disabled list, Wieters had been diagnosed with a partially torn ligament in his elbow, which would eventually lead to Tommy John surgery and cause him to miss the rest of the year.

The loss of Wieters might have been devastating. Most outside observers doubted the Orioles could overcome the loss of their two-way All-Star catcher. For the next 34 games, during which the Orioles went 15–19, that forecast appeared accurate. As it turned out, it was just another of the challenges the team would overcome.

On May 30, the Orioles finished their third and final four-game losing streak. Then the pitching staff kicked in, with Tillman providing stability at the top of the rotation, with Wei-Yin Chen, Bud Norris, Miguel Gonzalez, and Kevin Gausman settling in behind him. Zach Britton took over as the bullpen closer, with Tommy Hunter returning to his previous role as setup man, while Darren O'Day, Brian Matusz, and T. J. McFarland continued to provide the depth that had been so prominent in 2013.

When Wieters went down, Duquette immediately brought in veteran Nick Hundley, obtained in a trade with San Diego, to team with rookie Caleb Joseph behind the plate. The two provided a smooth transition for a pitching staff that had become a force as the season headed into the stretch run.

With the Orioles now solidly entrenched as the leader in the AL East, and amid speculation that another starter was still needed, Duquette instead made

a bold move to strengthen the strongest part of his pitching staff—the bullpen. Beating the July 31 trade deadline by mere hours, Duquette acquired left-hander Andrew Miller from the Red Sox in exchange for highly regarded minor league prospect Eduardo Rodriguez.

Suddenly, just when it appeared everything was in place for a deep run into October, the Orioles endured another potentially devastating injury. On August 11, with his season barely four months old and finally completely healed from his 2013 injury, Machado went down in a heap at home plate after swinging and fouling off a pitch. He suffered a partially torn ligament in his right knee, the same injury he endured in his left knee almost a year before, and was lost for the rest of the season.

The Orioles were 68–50 and led the Blue Jays by six games and the Yankees by eight when Machado's year ended. It presented one final chance for the Orioles to succumb to adversity, but they responsed by following the same script that they had throughout this injury-plagued, unforgettable year: The O's went 28–16 the rest of the way.

From May 31, when they were 26–27 and in third place, the Orioles went 70–39 to finish with a 96–66 record and win the AL East by 12 games. Every time a player was lost, Showalter's team somehow managed not only to survive but to improve its record. One obvious reason was the continued excellence on defense, where shortstop J. J. Hardy provided the kind of veteran leadership that enabled Schoop to take advantage of his defensive skills and stay in the lineup (hitting 16 home runs). It is no accident that for the second straight year the Orioles allowed the fewest amount of unearned runs in the major leagues, 36.

Cruz led the league with 40 home runs and drove in 108 runs to earn Most Valuable Oriole honors, but there were many contributors to the cause: Jones

OPPOSITE: Acquired in a February 2008 trade that sent lefty Erik Bedard to Seattle for five players including center fielder Adam Jones, Chris Tillman bounced between Triple AAA Norfolk and the Orioles for three and a half seasons before establishing himself in the starting rotation in July 2012. After going 9–3 with a 2.93 ERA over the second half of that season, he went 16–7 in 2013 and was named to the AL All-Star team. In 2014 he allowed three earned runs or fewer in 29 of his league-leading 34 starts and went 13–6 with a 3.34 ERA.

ABOVE: After a September call-up in 2013, rookie Jonathan Schoop established himself as slick defensive second baseman in 2014. The Curacao native also hit 16 homers.

finished with 29 home runs and 96 RBIs while hitting .281; Pearce took advantage of the opportunity to play regularly for the first time and responded with career highs in home runs (21), RBIs (49), and batting average (.293); and Delmon Young proved to be another of Duquette's off-season minor league contract steals, hitting .302 with seven homers and 30 RBIs as a part-time player. And although Davis's home run total dropped from 53 to 26, the Orioles hit 211 home runs to lead the major leagues for the second straight year.

But even given the deserved accolades for the O's offense and defense, pitching was the biggest difference in this team over the previous two years. In 2013, the team's earned run average of 4.20 was 23rd in the major leagues and 10th in the American League. A year later, the 3.43 ERA ranked seventh in the major leagues and third best in the AL.

Those numbers spoke volumes about the improvement of relatively young pitchers like Tillman, Chen, Norris, and Gonzalez. The team's 1.24 WHIP (or combined walks plus hits per inning pitched) was third best in the league. "Sometimes it's better to just let them figure it out for themselves," said Wallace,

ABOVE: The third player selected in the 2010 draft, Manny Machado was in his third minor league season as shortstop when he was brought up from Double A Bowie and installed as the Orioles third baseman on August 9, 2012. He quickly established himself as a defensive wizard at third base, winning a Gold Glove in his first full season in 2013. His bat proved potent, too, as he led the AL with 51 doubles while batting .283 with 14 homers—at the tender age of twenty-one. It appeared the only thing that could slow him down was himself; a 2013 left knee injury got his 2014 season off to a late start, and a similar injury to his right knee in August 2014 caused him to miss half the season.

deflecting any credit back to his pitchers, who nevertheless heaped praise on the pitching coach and on Chiti, his bullpen assistant.

Whereas in 2012, earning a wild-card spot in the postseason and ending a fourteen-year losing streak was considered a major breakthrough, it was different this time around. There was much more on the plate, and when the Orioles clinched their first division title in seventeen years with an 8–2 win over the Blue Jays on September 16, the reaction was predictable—long and loud, with an orange-clad crowd of 34,297 joining the celebration, which went on for more than an hour after the game ended.

"It's an awesome experience," said Nick Markakis, who had spent his entire career in an Orioles' uniform and was on the disabled list with a broken wrist during the Orioles' playoff run in 2012. "To do it with these guys . . . it's one of the reasons I wanted to be part of this team and this organization."

One note of irony about the clinching victory came from the fact that Ubaldo Jimenez, whose season had been viewed as a disappointment, was the winning pitcher. "I wanted to find a way to get this team a win," said Jimenez.

The electric atmosphere wasn't lost on the players or their manager. "It was a great environment," said Hunter, who was on the mound for the last out. "It was really loud . . . these guys love baseball . . . these fans, this city."

After taking in much of the celebration from a distance, Showalter tried to assess his feelings. "This place is special," he said. "I'm biased, but I don't think there's any more electric place than this ballpark when something's on the line for the city of Baltimore. I told Dave (Wallace) during the national anthem, 'Just wait until the playoffs.' "

Showalter was right, of course, as he had been about just about everything else since taking over as manager on August 2, 2010. For the first two games of the Division Series, "electric" seemed like a mild adjective to describe the atmosphere at Camden Yards, as the Orioles took a 2–0 lead en route to a three-game sweep of the Tigers.

The noise level reached a boisterous crescendo when Young delivered a pinch-hit, bases-loaded double to drive in the winning run in the eighth inning of Game 2 of the ALDS. The crowd reaction, which exploded over an area of several blocks, was gauged by veteran observers to be the loudest ever in the Camden Yards area.

The celebratory mood continued into the American League Championship Series; unfortunately, although the atmosphere remained the same, the result would be different. A pair of painful two-run losses at home to the Royals, followed by a pair of excruciating 2–1 defeats in Kansas City, brought a highly successful season to an abrupt halt.

It took awhile for the sudden conclusion to register. "My emotion right now is for the players, the organization, and the fans, and I keep thinking if there was something I or we could have done different," said Showalter, groping for words to explain his feelings. "If you care, like our people care, it hurts. I know how much it hurts these guys.

"Our fans have been there, ownership has been there, and we feel bad about disappointing them," Showalter added, before quickly shifting gears from the past to the future. "So, now, we'll start over again."

The 2014 season came up one step short of the World Series, but like the previous sixty years in the Baltimore Orioles' story, it was a remarkable journey, one that had to be negotiated over numerous bumps along the way. Still, it seemed like more of a beginning, or perhaps a continuation, than an ending.

BELOW: Pinch-hitter Delmon Young delivers a bases-clearing double to give the Orioles an 8-7 lead in the seventh inning of Game 2 of the 2014 AL Division Series against the Tigers. Young batted .302 in a part-time role during the season, including .500 (10-for-20) as a pinch-hitter.
FOLLOWING PAGES: Adam Jones shares the AL East Championship pennant with some of the 35,297 fans who came to Camden Yards on September 16, 2014, when the Orioles beat the Blue Jays to clinch the first title on their home field since 1979.

CENTRIC
SINESS SYSTEMS
SHARP
Bring in the Closer!
RIDE MTA!
AFTER THE GAME,
KEEP PLAYING
HORSESHOE
BALTIMORE
HorseshoeBaltimore.com
RIGHT ON LEE ST.
LEFT ON RUSSELL ST.

MEMORABLE GAMES
2011–2014

September 28, 2011

Twice down to their last strike in the season's final game, Chris Davis and Nolan Reimold hit doubles and Robert Andino follows with a game-winning single as the Orioles beat Boston, 4–3, helping to eliminate the Red Sox from postseason play.

May 10, 2012

The Orioles tie an AL record when Ryan Flaherty, J. J. Hardy, and Nick Markakis lead off the game with back-to-back-to-back home runs in a 6–5 win over the Rangers at Camden Yards, one night after Texas' Josh Hamilton had hit four home runs against the Birds.

May 6, 2012

Chris Davis goes 0-for-8 as the DH, but with the Orioles out of available pitchers, he takes the mound and gets the win with two innings of scoreless relief as the Orioles beat the Red Sox, 9–6, at Fenway Park. Davis, the ninth Oriole pitcher of the game, gets Darnell McDonald to hit into a game-ending double play after Adam Jones's three-run homer off McDonald put the Birds ahead in the top of the 17th inning.

August 10, 2012

One night after going 2-for-4 with a triple in his major league debut, Manny Machado cracks two homers and drives in four runs in a 7–1 win over the Royals at Camden Yards, becoming the first player ever to record a triple and two homers in his first two big-league games. Playing third base after being called up from Double- A Bowie, where he was playing shortstop, Machado stabilizes the infield and the Orioles go 33–18 with him in the lineup the rest of the season.

September 6, 2012

With a sellout crowd of 46,298 on hand to see Cal Ripken's statue unveiled, the Yankees score five runs in the top of the eighth inning to tie the game before Adam Jones, Mark Reynolds, and Chris Davis all homer in the bottom of the inning to give the Orioles a 10–6 win and a share of the AL East lead.

September 16, 2014

The Orioles beat Toronto, 8–2, to win their first AL East title in seventeen years. Most of the 35,000 fans at Camden Yards stay for more than an hour to celebrate the team's first title clinch at home since 1979.

September 17, 2013

Chris Davis's 51st home run of the season—a new club record—ties the game, and the Orioles go on to beat the Red Sox, 3–2, at Fenway Park. Davis finishes the season with 53 homers, leading the majors in homers and RBIs (138).

September 30, 2012

The Orioles beat the Red Sox, 6–3, in their home finale as Jim Johnson records his 50th save; he would finish the season with a club-record 51 saves. Afterward, the players join 41,257 fans to watch a scoreboard broadcast of the Angels-Rangers doubleheader. An Angels comeback in the first game delays the Orioles' playoff berth—but only for a few hours, as the Angels lose the nightcap to Texas.

September 14, 2014

For the second time in three days, the Orioles get a walk-off win over the Yankees. Nelson Cruz, Steve Pearce, and Kelly Johnson all double in the ninth to beat New York, 3–2, in front of 43,947 fans, and lead the AL East by 11½ games.

October 5, 2012

The Orioles win the first-ever AL "play-in" wild-card game against the Rangers in Texas, 5–1. Joe Saunders, acquired on August 26, allows one run in 5 2/3 innings for the win. The Orioles eventually fall in five games to the Yankees in the AL Division Series.

October 3, 2014

With the Orioles trailing, 6–3, in the eighth inning, a Camden Yards crowd of 48,058 goes wild when Delmon Young's pinch-hit three-run double caps a four-run inning to beat the Tigers, 7–6, in Game 2 of the ALCS.

BALTIMORE ORIOLES
Chairman of the Board / CEO: Peter Angelos
Executive Vice President: John Angelos
Vice President, Communications & Marketing: Greg Bader
Director, Orioles Alumni / Project Editor: Bill Stetka
Team Photographer: Todd Olszewski
Photography Assistant: Matt Hazlett

Special thanks to Sports Legends Museum and past Orioles photographers Mort Tadder, Jerry Wachter,
Jay Spencer, Neil Leifer, and Marshall Janoff; Orioles Alumni interns Kevin Cohen and Nicole Gould for editorial assistance; and
Kristen Schultz, Lacey Brauer, and Amanda Sarver of the Orioles for their assistance in developing and promoting this project.

INSIGHT
EDITIONS

PO Box 3088
San Rafael, CA 94912
www.insighteditions.com

Find us on Facebook: www.facebook.com/InsightEditions
Follow us on Twitter: @insighteditions

ISBN: 978-1-60887-318-0

INSIGHT EDITIONS
Publisher: Raoul Goff
Co-publisher: Michael Madden
Art Director: Chrissy Kwasnik
Interior Designer: Rachel Maloney
Jacket Designer: Chris Kosek
Acquisitions Manager: Steve Jones
Executive Editor: Vanessa Lopez
Project Editor: Dustin Jones
Production Editor: Rachel Anderson
Production Manager: Anna Wan

ROOTS of PEACE   REPLANTED PAPER

Insight Editions, in association with Roots of Peace, will plant two trees for each tree used in the manufacturing of this book.
Roots of Peace is an internationally renowned humanitarian organization dedicated to eradicating land mines worldwide
and converting war-torn lands into productive farms and wildlife habitats. Roots of Peace will plant two million fruit and nut
trees in Afghanistan and provide farmers there with the skills and support necessary for sustainable land use.

Manufactured in China by Insight Editions

10 9 8 7 6 5 4 3 2 1